I0106186

How would an architect design a house on Mars?

ANSWER: planet

-Albert B. Squid

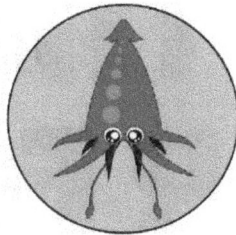

SQUARE ROOT OF SQUID PUBLISHING

BOOK CONCEPT BY: ALBERT B. SQUID
ILLUSTRATIONS/WRITING BY: ALBERT B. SQUID
COVER DESIGN BY: HANNES KLEIN/jkdtp

FOR SOME EXTRA STUFF THAT GOES WITH THIS BOOK SCAN THAT QR CODE OR FOLLOW THE LINK BELOW IT.

www.albertosquid.com

HEY ARCHITECT!

"THE SPACE AGENCY" has hired us once again architect, but this time, to design a house on Mars for four astronauts to live in and do research. That's right architect, you heard that right...ON MARS!!! The astronauts filled out the order form on the next page to let us know what kind of house they would like. So if you are ready architect, LET'S GET TO IT!!!

ORDER FORM

NAME Harris Georgetown, Joan Lemon
Rodrigo Starsky, Paula MacArthur (astronauts)

SITE LOCATION Mars

HOUSE STYLE mobile/stationary

PROJECT BUDGET 1,000,000,000 cryptos

HOUSE SIZE For two couples

HOUSE REQUIRMENTS We're two astronaut couples and would like our individual homes but we would like them to connect to a a common space with lab, office, rec room cafeteria, garden, observation room, gym

THE SITE

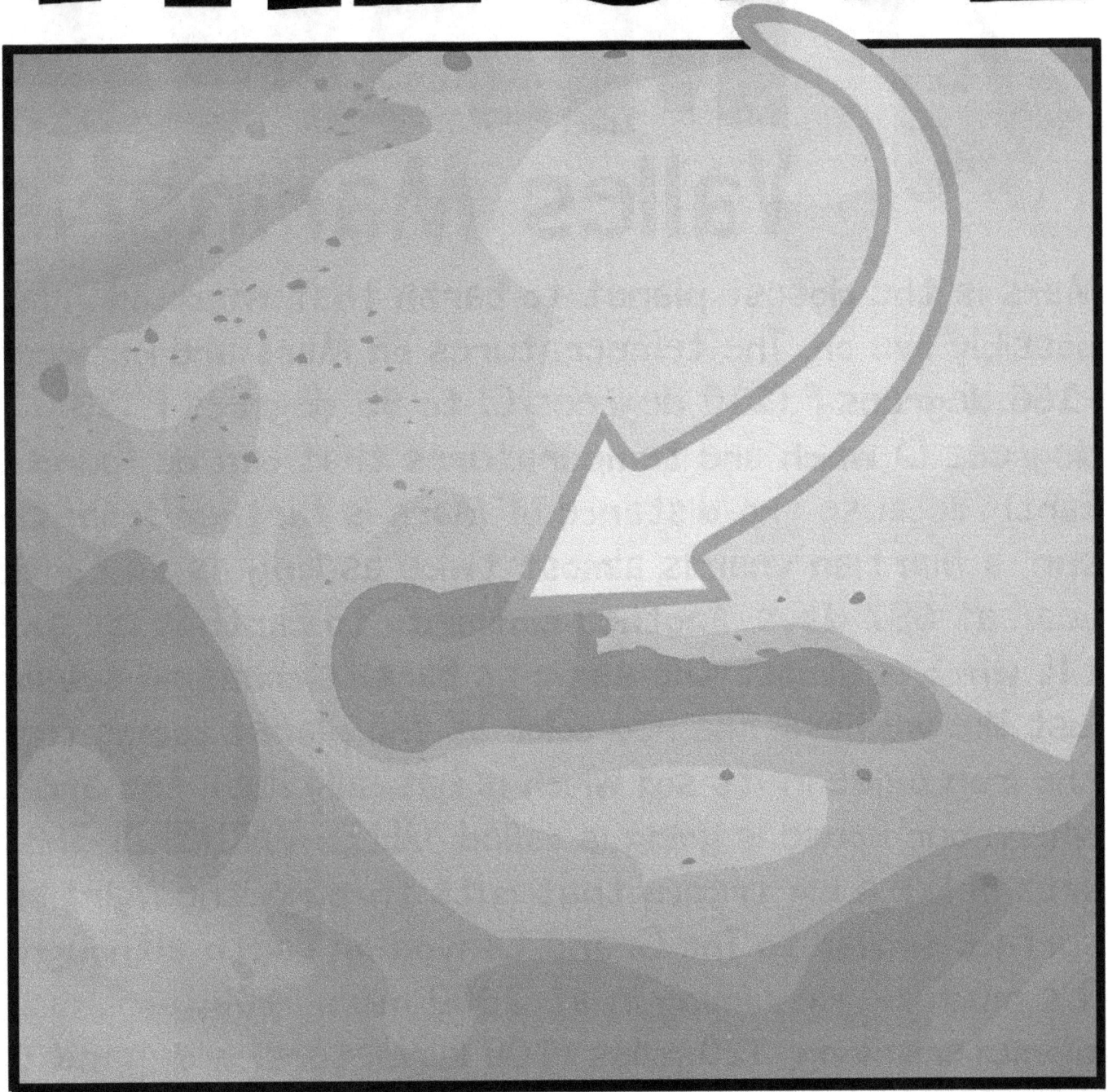

MARS

Valles Marineris 13.9°S 59.2°W

All About MARS
Valles Marineris

Mars is the closest planet to Earth that we could possibly live on. The temperatures on Mars are between -166 degrees F (110 degrees C) to 95 degrees F (35 degrees C) which are temperatures that can be found on Earth. Because the distance of Mars is farther from the sun, a Martian year is almost twice as long as an Earth year at 687 days. Another similarity to Earth is its axis tilt which is almost the same as Earth's creating seasons just like we have. The red color of the planet comes from the iron oxide in its soil which is basically RUST. The area where our house is going is called VALLES MARINERIS. This area is like a big trench that cuts through the Martian surface similar to The Grand Canyon on Earth although it's much bigger coming in at 2500 miles (4000 kilometers) long, 120 miles (200 kilometers) wide, and 5 miles (7 kilometers) deep. This is a great choice for our site because scientists think this area has a lot of stuff our astronauts will need to live including ice (which is water), that can be used to sustain life, grow plants, and extract oxygen.

THINGS WE'RE GONNA NEED

Here's a list of things we're gonna need to make this Mars house work. Can you write down how we can supply these things?

1. WATER (How do we get it?)

_____

_____

2. POWER/ELECTRICITY (How do we get it?)

_____

_____

3. OXYGEN (How do we get it?)

_____

_____

THE CONCEPT

Ok architect this is the beginning point of designing our house. This is where we brainstorm and sketch all the ideas that come to mind (no matter how weird these ideas are 'cause anything goes at this stage and the stranger the better, I always say. LOL) about what needs to happen to get an idea of how we are gonna design a RAD house that is everything our clients want, plus a concept that ties it all together. So as we sketch let's think of things the clients' asked for and at the same time the conditions of the site like where light comes from. Maybe there are mountains and we echo the roof shape to look like that. Maybe the area is populated by man-eating alien space bugs and we design a floor plan that follows the shape of their bodies. Remember there are no crazy ideas here. So let's get to sketchin' shall we architect?

THE ARCHITECT'S UNIFORM

Hey architect, if you feel like it, color in the bow tie & eyeglasses, tape 'em together, and wear 'em before we start the job.

fold the glasses
arms on the line
and tape/glue
here

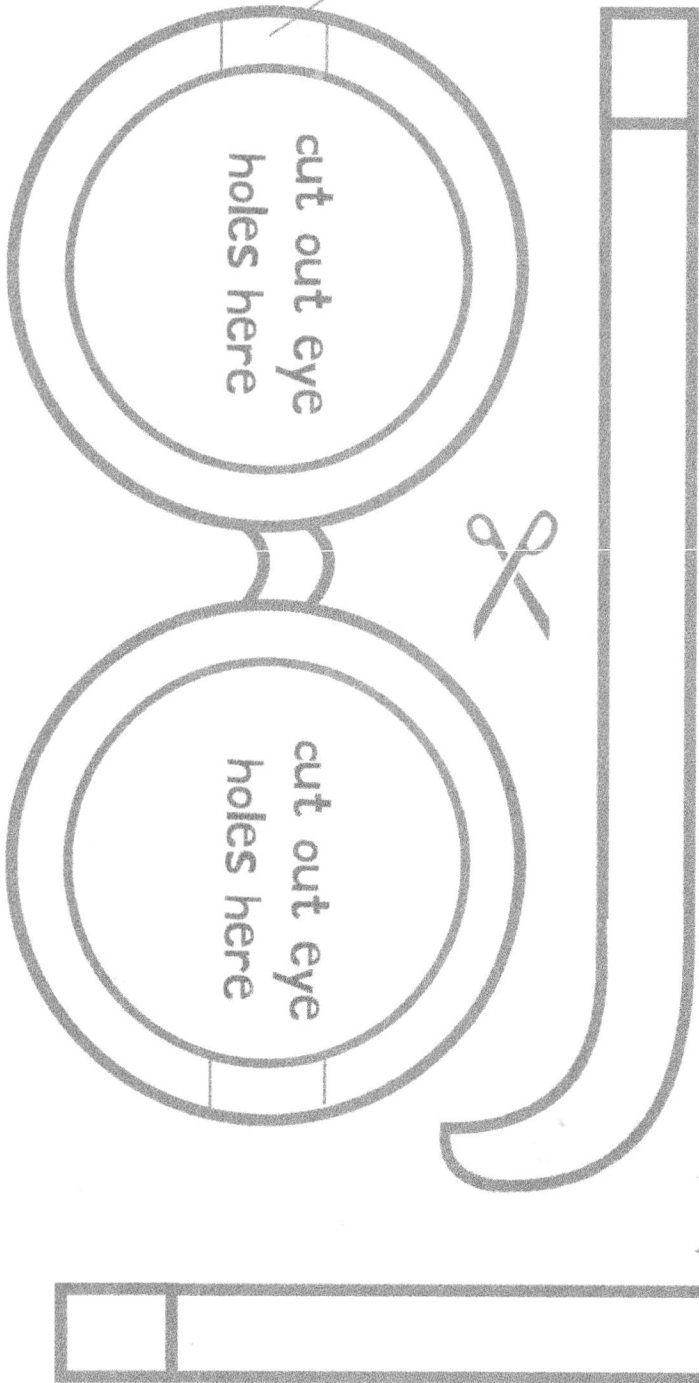

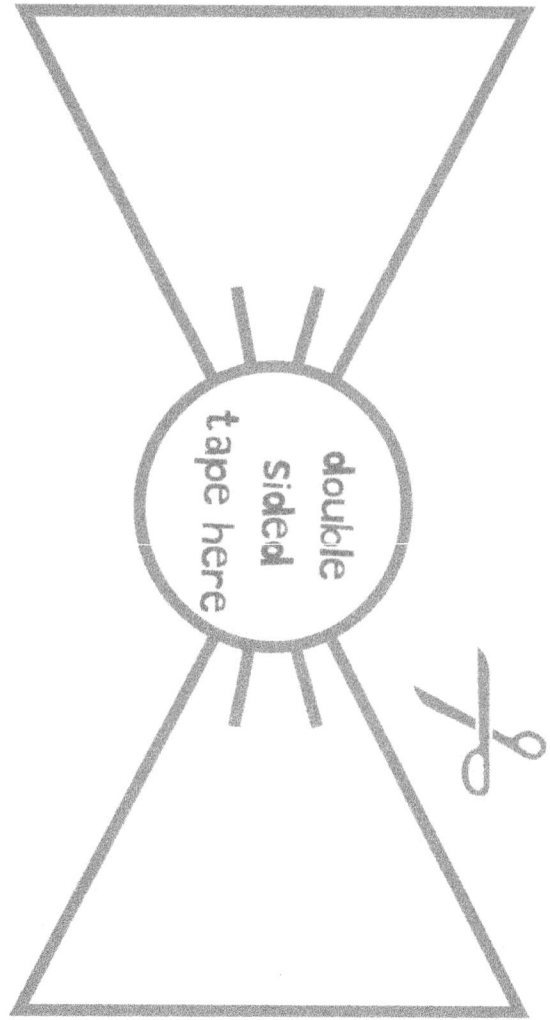

cut out eye
holes here

cut out eye
holes here

double
sided
tape here

OUR HOUSE DESIGN

SKETCH BOOK

a spaceship or an avocado?

Mars House

wheels=mobile

rock=stationary

bee=mobile

hive=stationary

Things the astronauts asked for.

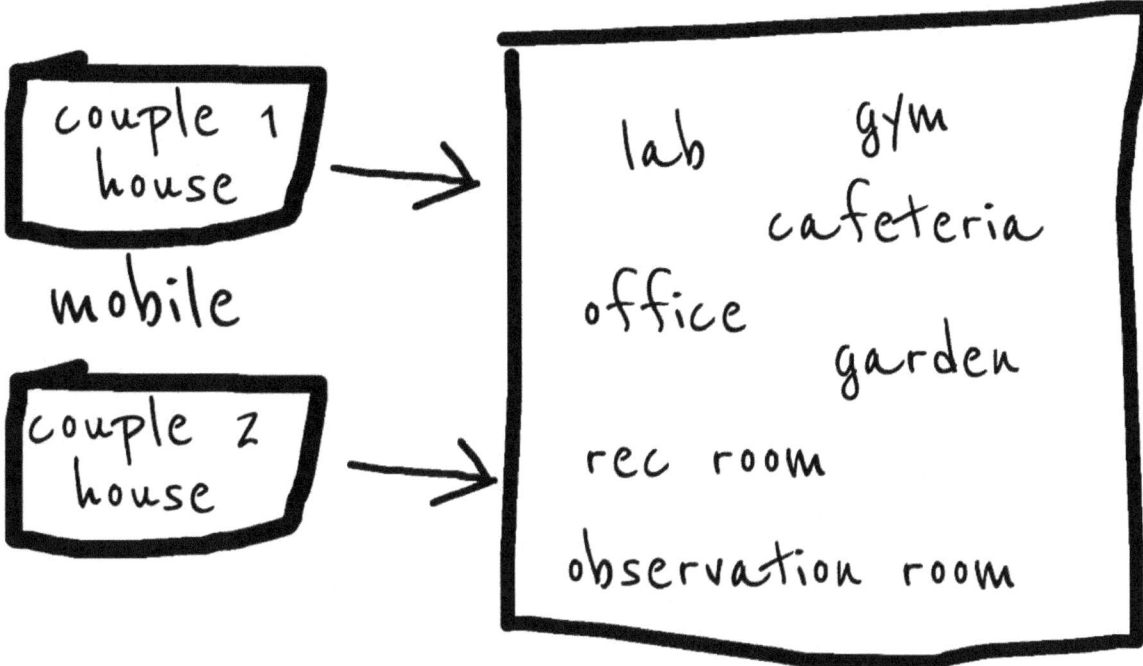

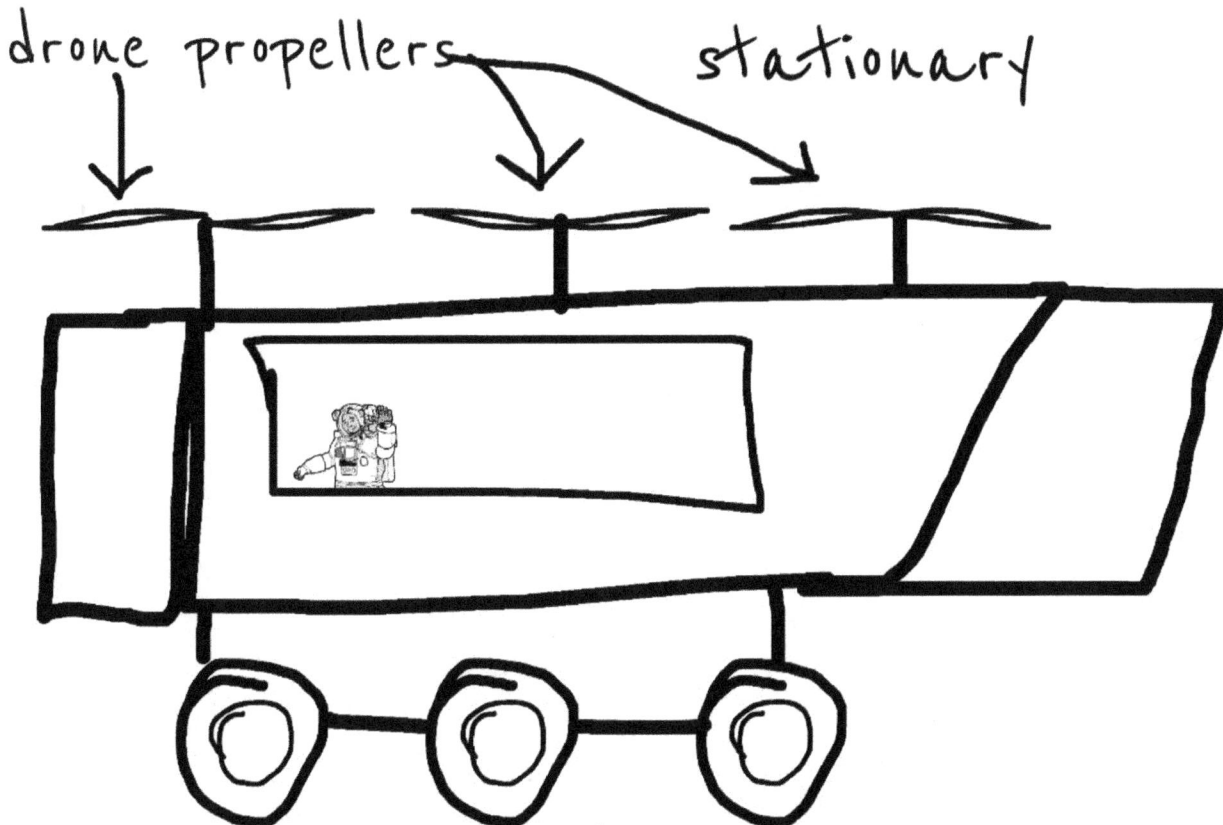

couple 1
house

mobile

couple 2
house

lab gym
cafeteria
office
garden
rec room
observation room

drone propellers   stationary

Mars RV Mobile Home

Your turn again architect!

add your ideas right here on this page.

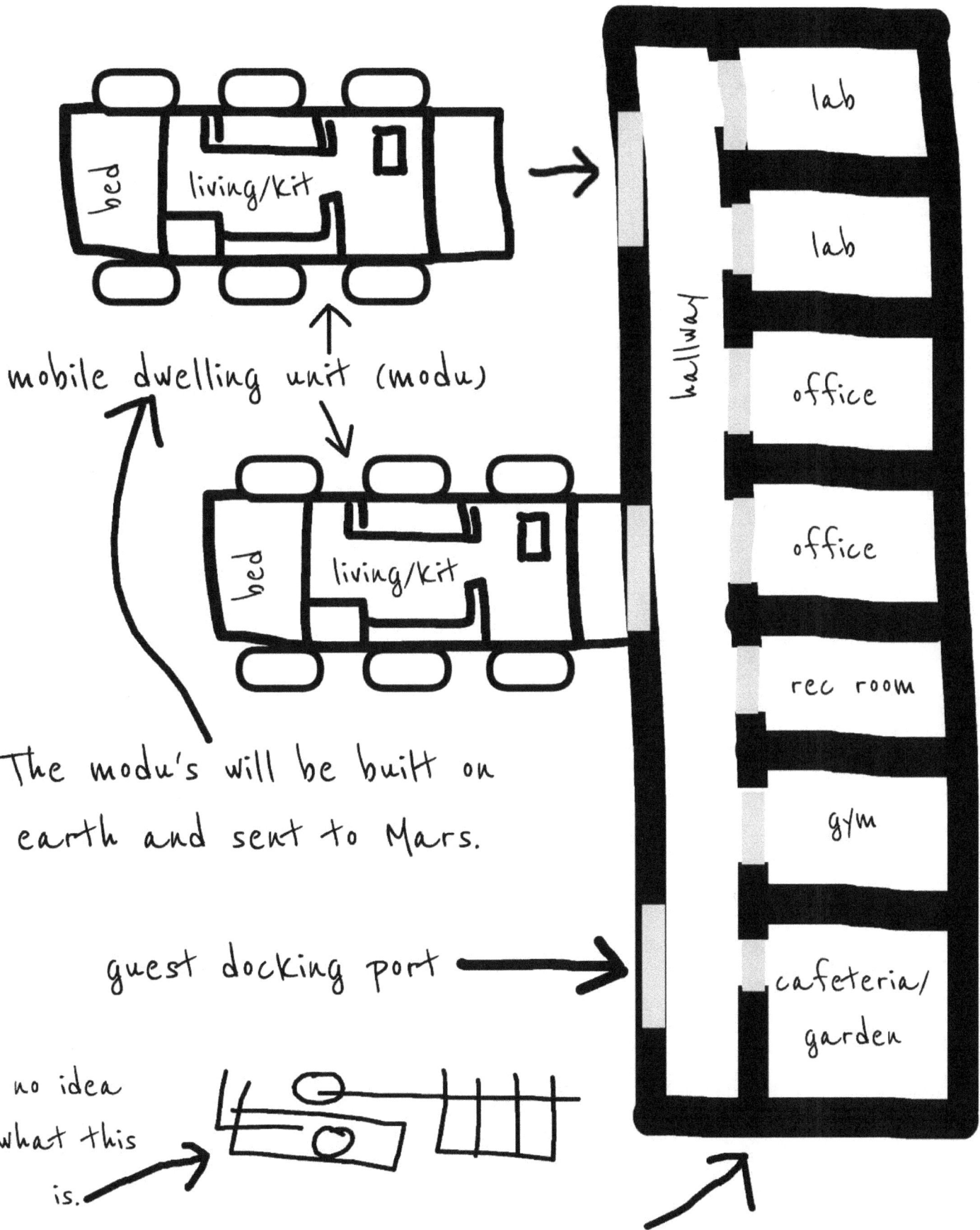

bed

living/kit

mobile dwelling unit (modu)

bed

living/kit

lab

lab

office

office

rec room

gym

cafeteria/ garden

hallway

The modu's will be built on earth and sent to Mars.

guest docking port

no idea what this is.

The stationary building will be like an airport and this will be built first by robots using Mars soil (regolith).

Your turn again architect!

add your ideas right here on this page.

Draw some more floor plan ideas here and then we shall move on to house placement and elevation drawings.

Before the astronauts go to Mars we have to send some stuff first!

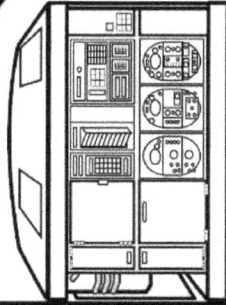

1. We need a Mars soil melter to make concrete.

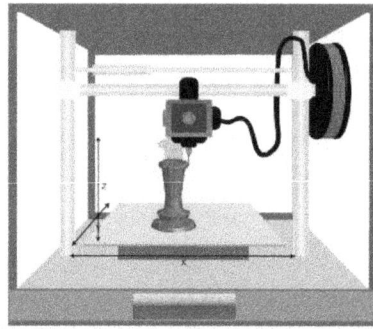

2. We add the martian concrete to a 3D printer to make the Mars house shapes.

3. We use robots to lift and move things into place before the astronauts get there.

See if you can lay out the floor plan a little better than me right here on this page so we can start to draw the elevations.

Let's start to figure out what this port looks like on the outside with elevation drawings.

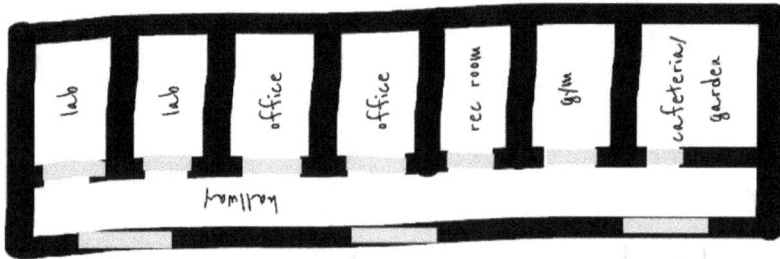

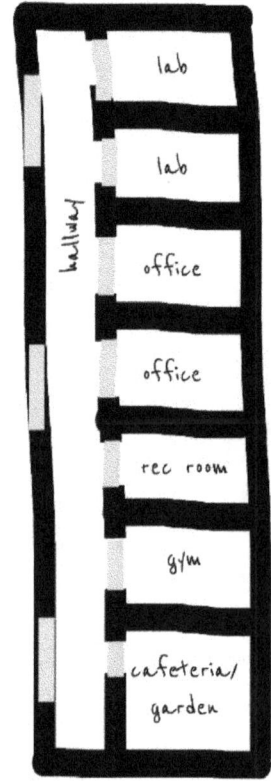

lab | lab | office | office | rec room | gym | cafeteria/garden

hallway

lab
lab
office
office
rec room
gym
cafeteria/garden

hallway

Reminder: We draw some lines from the floor plan to the elevation to know where things go.

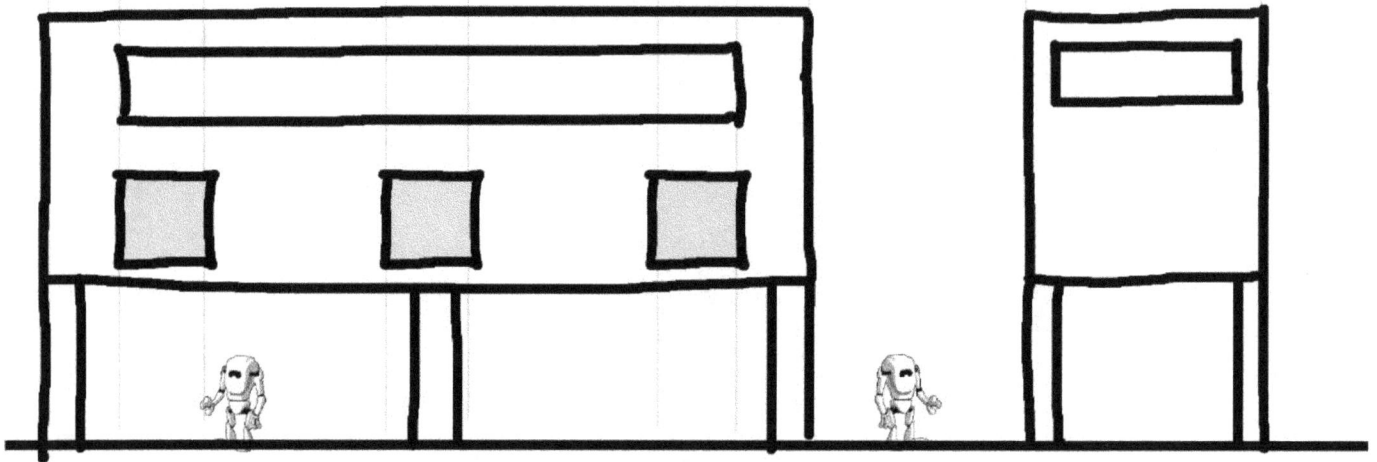

Let's start with the part of the house that the robots will build, "The Port"

Now, let's do the same thing with the MODU section that will be built on earth by humans and sent to Mars.

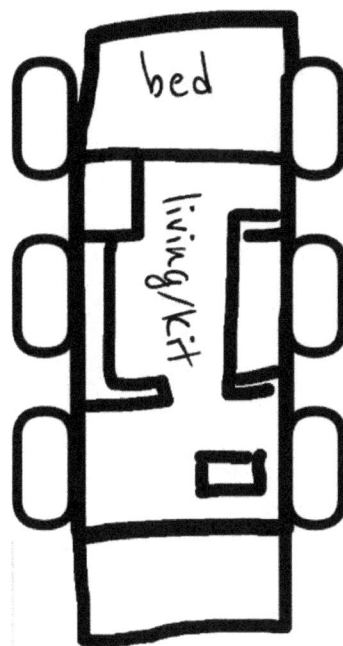

bed

living/kit

bed

living/kit

This MODU has wheels for driving on the ground and propellers so it can fly too!

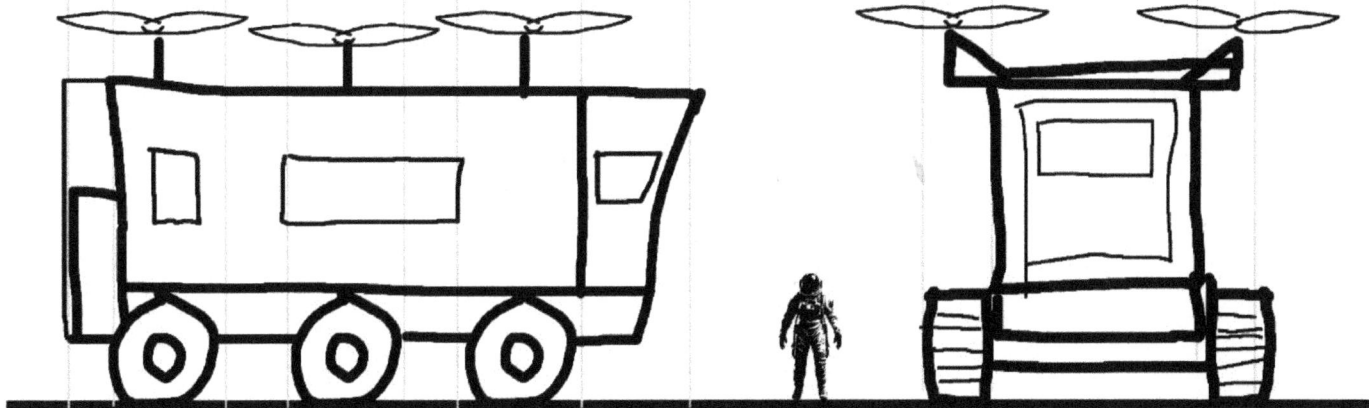

My drawings are pretty basic. If you wanna add your own spin on the elevations, draw 'em right here on this page.

Last chance to add concept sketches here.

MARS WORDS

REGOLITH: This is basically Mars dirt and can be used to make something like concrete.

MARSQUAKE: Like an earthquake on Earth, a marsquake shakes the Martian ground.

PERSEVERANCE: A robotic rover that was sent to Mars to gather data and send it back to Earth.

OLYMPUS MONS: The largest volcano on Mars and the largest volcano in the Solar System.

PHOBOS: The larger of the two moons of Mars. The word comes from the Greek God of fear.

DEIMOS: The smaller of the two moons of Mars. The word comes from the Greek God of terror.

MARTIAN: Someone or something that is from the planet Mars.

Can you find all the Mars words from the left page in this puzzle below? If so, circle them!

```
H M T D S J V D E I M O S S P
Z N V K W T L M B E H V N E L
R D V X X D H Y S J P X C X M
U O A D V I Q M V F H W U F J
O V O L Y M P U S M O N S N A
Y R G H X L R Q S Y G I M R W
H R B D K X I N R N W R F R G
L R Y N L I W E Z A Y K U F R
K B E J W B E C W R F W Z H F
I O X Z M Z I P R I E Y I C M
L O Q E A K K E F R D F C R U
R D K D I J F M H I Q T F E Q
V P B E Z E F Q J K P H S G Y
Q V E V A S S A P D W S Q O Y
I Z I R N D O C P Z M O P L F
T M U W D E J Z F W G C K I H
Y A A B E Y V D Z E A B G T D
O C K R Y B C E O R P B H H Q
T D L V B I N E L X M R W V P
K Y O P I G A K R K E A F S D
M P S T G Z Z I P A P J W T O
A R J U Z Z I N J X N O L D C
R K K B V T T D R U F C Z D P
S H V S N S O Z H S Q Z E N S
Q U D M F J Y K K Z F P D O J
U A H O P J W J P Z T D B P D
A B Z H H E J N N X J O A W A
K U H H H L B J L O H V W N B
E A X V V R U C L P L I M Y M
Z A Y L L T U L C E C Q E Y B
```

THE FLOOR PLANS

So, architect, this is the part where we really figure out the layout of the rooms and how everything flows together in more detail. Think of a floor plan like you cut the roof off the building and are looking down at it like you are a bird. You can see all the rooms, doors, walls, and windows from up there. On the following pages are some things that get put in floor plans. How rad is that?

We should now make a list of things that will go in our floor plan. I wrote the first one. Can you fill in the rest architect?

1. Draw in the walls, windows, and doors.

2. _____

3. _____

4. _____

5. _____

6. _____

7. _____

SOME THINGS WE USE IN FLOOR PLANS

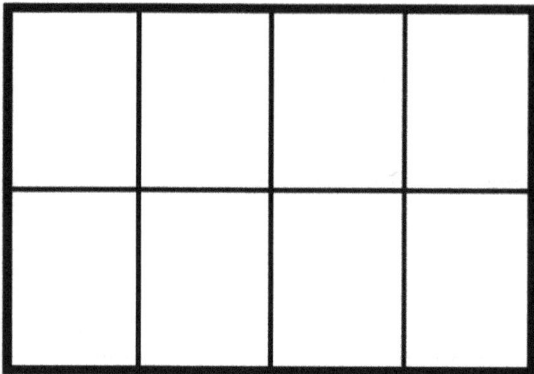

This is stairs in a floor plan

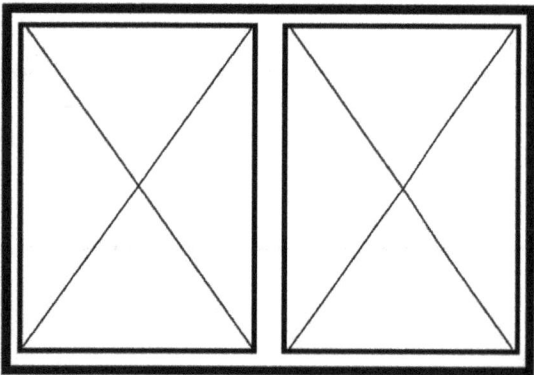

This is an elevator

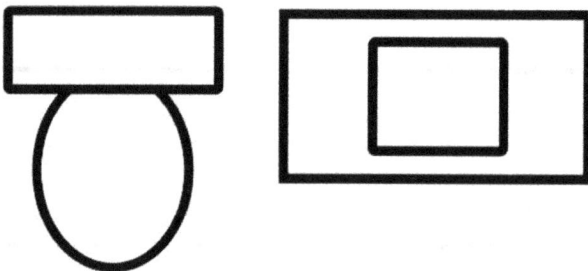

This is a toilet and sink

SOME THINGS WE USE IN FLOOR PLANS

This is a **door** in a floor plan

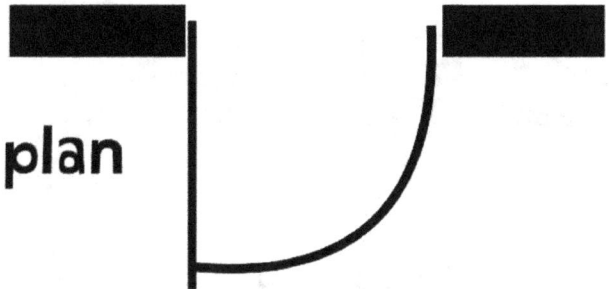

This is a **window**

This is a **wall opening**

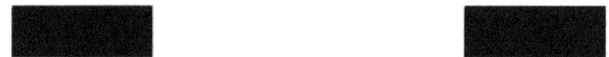

This is where the wall and **column** meet

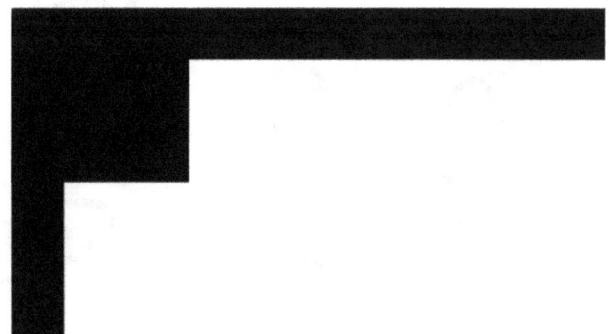

SOME THINGS WE USE IN FLOOR PLANS

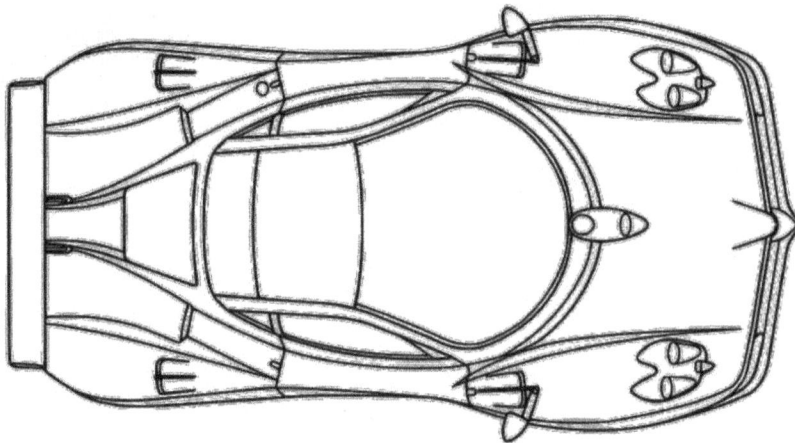

Cars can go in floor plans

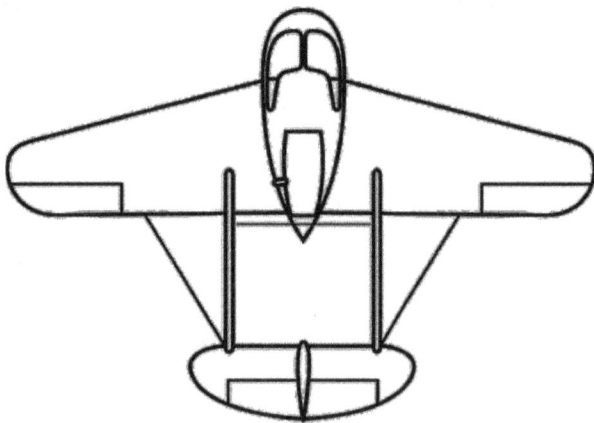

And so can planes

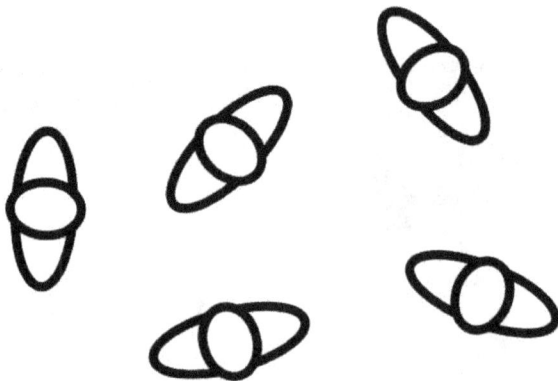

Even people

SOME THINGS WE USE IN FLOOR PLANS

This is a bed in a floor plan

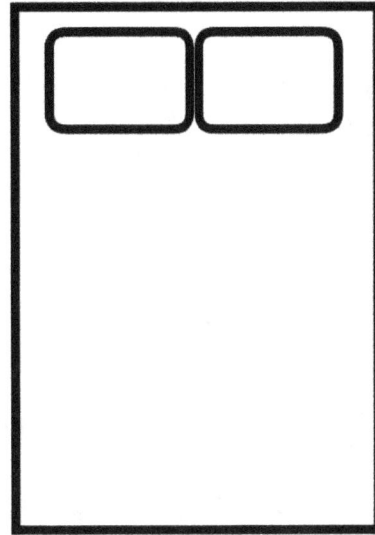

This is chairs and a table

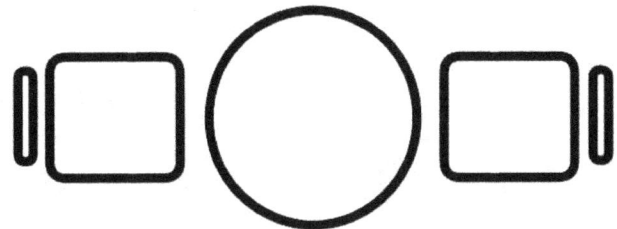

This is a sofa

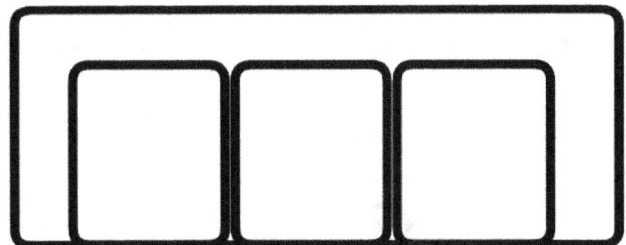

SCALE

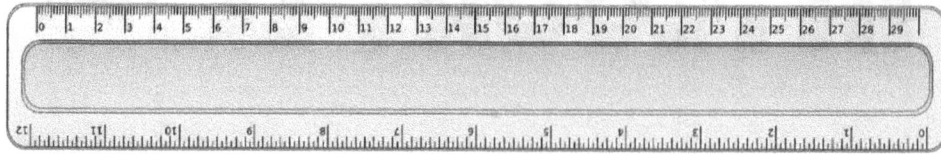

As you know architect, scale is the size of the structure compared to the people that use it and the things around it. If our rooms are too big, the house might not feel cozy, too small would make it uncomfortable. This is where we use measurements to figure out the dimensions of the house. But I'll leave that up to you architect. You can fill in the amount for widths and lengths as you see fit. Another way to sense the scale of a building is by actually drawing people or objects in the floor plan or standing next to an elevation or section drawing.

Here is a simple example of scale. Because you kinda already know these common items, when you put 'em together you could probably easily guess the different sizes of these things. Give it a try! Fill in how big you think these things are.

BIRD:_____

CAT:_____

PERSON:_____

HOUSE:_____

1 square = 3 ft (1 m)

LEVEL 1

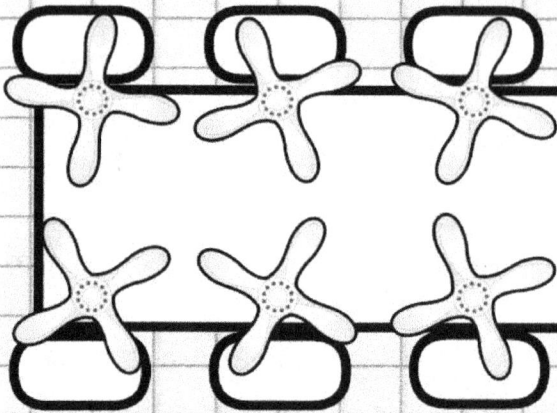

guest dock/
supply drop

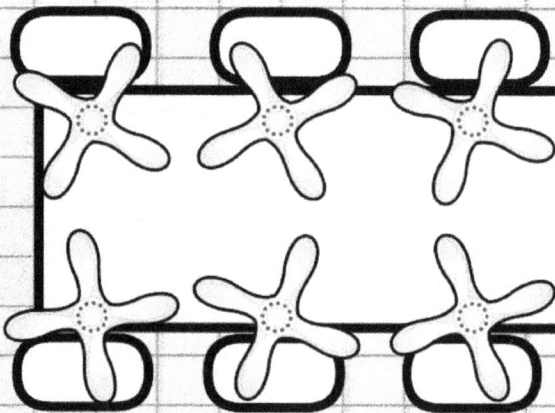

Add room names,
furniture and/or
fixtures to the PORT's
floor plan.

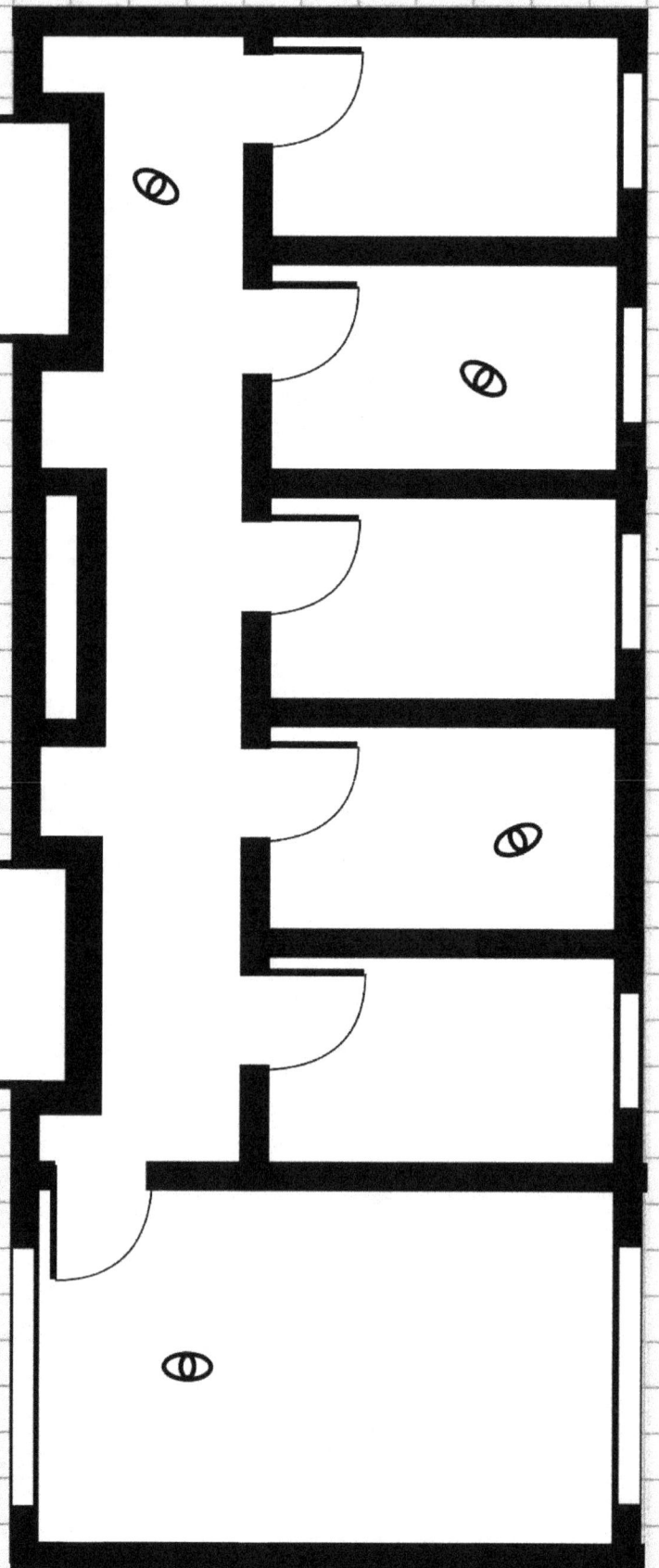

1 square = 3 ft (1 m)

opening to level 1

LEVEL 2

Hey architect! You have this huge space upstairs to do whatever you want. Would you add walls? Windows? Doors? Furniture? It's entirely up to you.

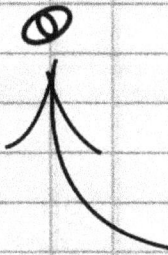

This is looking down on an astronaut.

1 square = 1 ft (.3 m)

MOBILE DWELLING UNIT (MODU)

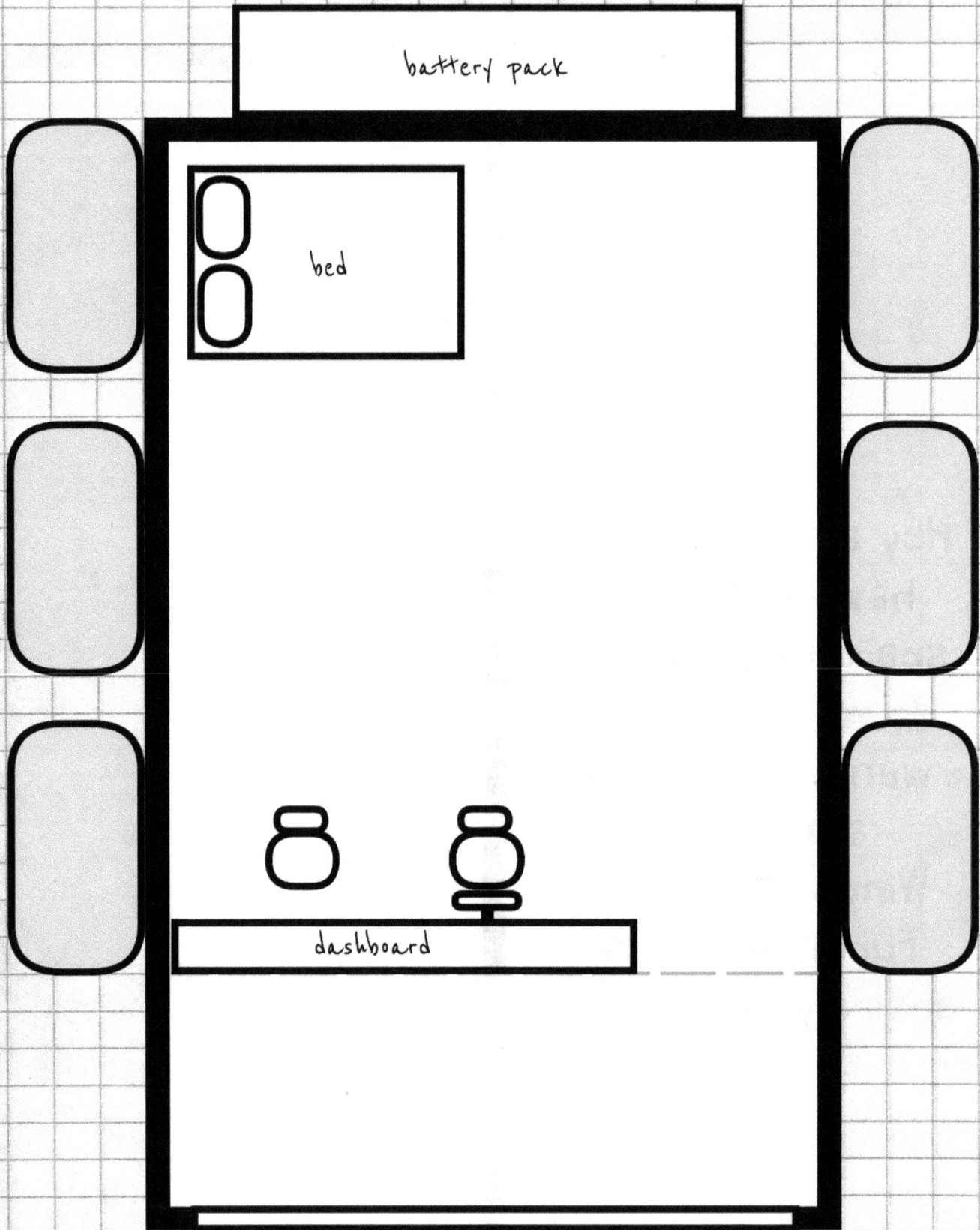

battery pack

bed

dashboard

Can you add the bathroom, kitchen, and living room architect?

1 square = 5 ft (1.5 m)

Maybe you have a completely different idea for a floor plan architect, if so draw it here.

THE ROBOTS HAVE ARRIVED!

So architect! The rocket with the robots, regolith soil melter, and 3D printer has just landed on Mars to start building "THE PORT" before the astronauts show up with the MODU's. There is one small problem though. The SPACE AGENCY made some wrong calculations and the rocket landed 5,000 KLICKS away from our building site at VALLES MARINERIS. Can you find the right path to get the stuff to the site from that map over there on the right page?

ROCKET LANDING

VALLES MARINERIS

x-57483-3784-4328441111

ELEVATION DRAWINGS

We did some basic ones, but now let's improve them. These are the types of drawings that show what the outside of the building looks like. We should show each side of the building like we are standing in front of it looking straight at it from the north, south, east, and west sides.

With elevation drawings, we can start to figure out the scale of our house and how high the roof will be. Let's use our floor plan to help us with the first elevation drawing as we did with the concept sketches.

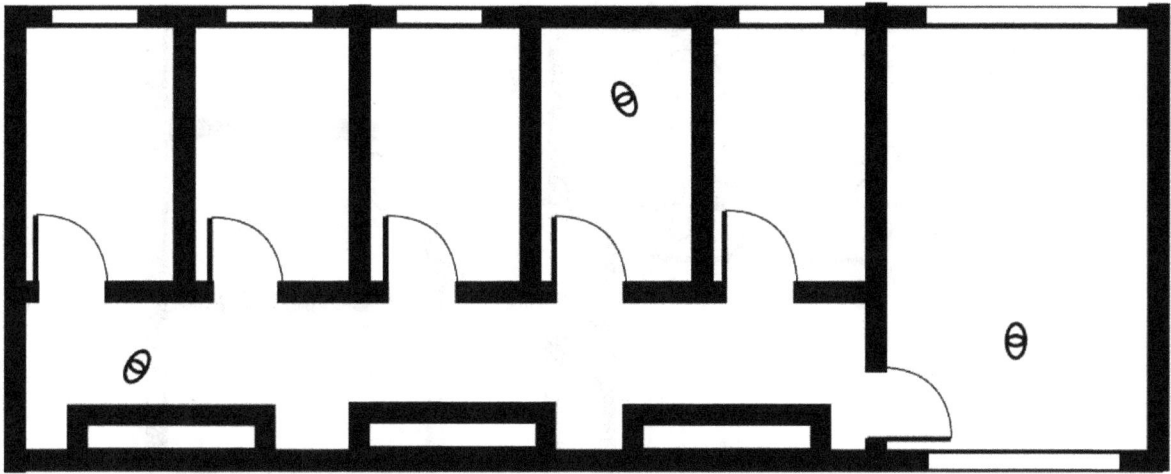

Let's put the port on stilts so
Mar's red dust blows under the
building so it does not get buried.

The Port Front Elevation

Here is a
side view
of The
Port and
The Modu
when they
are
connected.

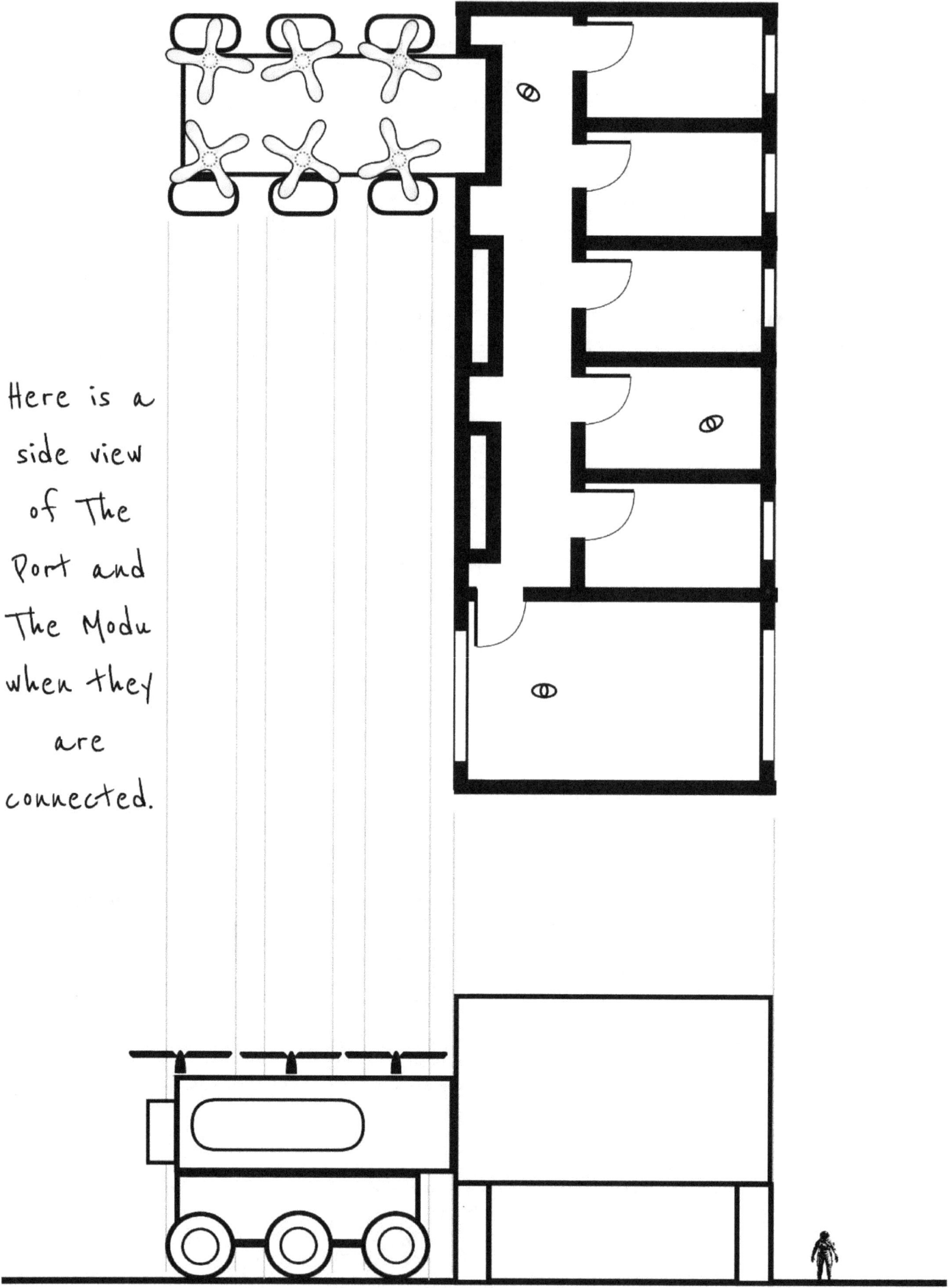

The Port Front Elevation

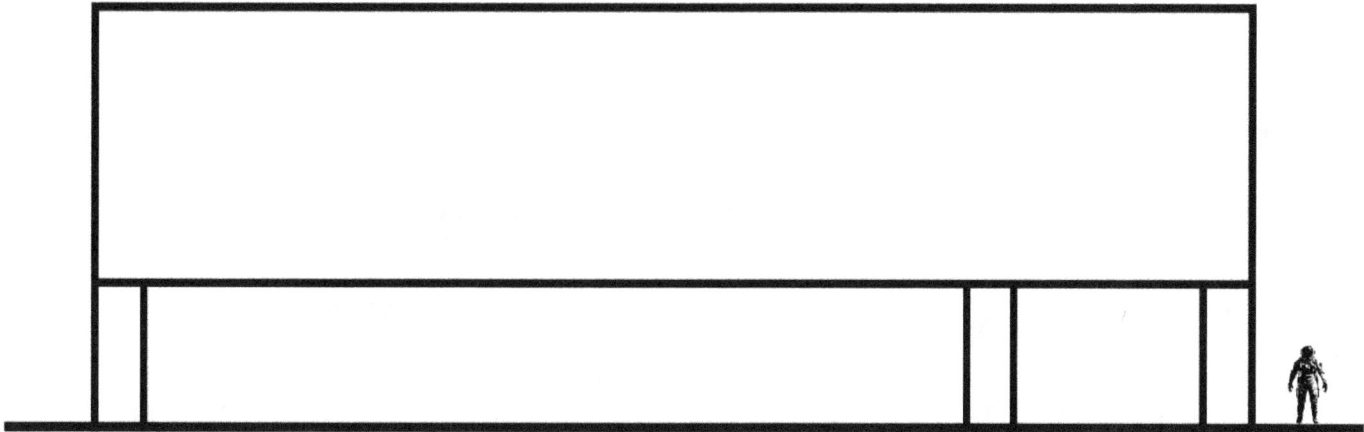

Would you draw the elevations differently architect? How would you design the look of the front and back of this building? Draw it right here!

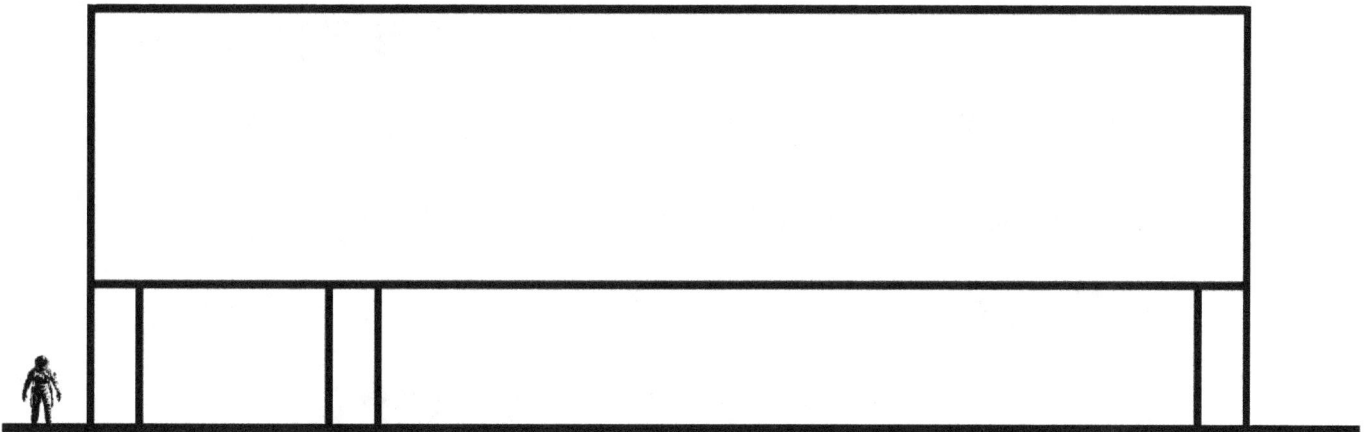

The Port Back Elevation

RENDERING

Thanks for helping me architect, this design is really coming along. So, there are some tricks to make our elevations pop off the page and that's rendering. With the side of our pencil, we can color in different shades of gray to show things further away or closer up. We can add shadows to give depth to edges, doors, windows, etc. We can put different size dots to show concrete or other wall finishes. We can draw thin lines to look like glass. But you knew that architect. Anyhoo, there's a small example on the right there to refresh your memory.

ELEVATION WITHOUT RENDERING

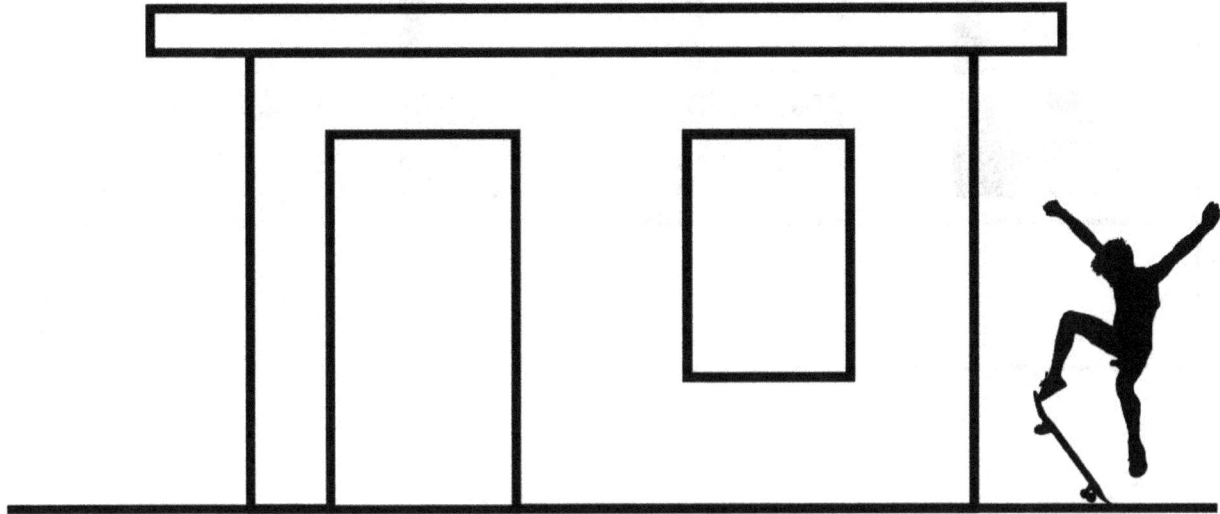

ELEVATION WITH RENDERING

sun coming from this side

The farther something sticks out or goes in, the bigger the shadow is, or the smaller the shadow is.

The Space Agency just called and want to have a meeting. I rendered the front of THE PORT but didn't have a chance to do the MODU. Can you add more details and render the MODU below.

Before starting the
CROSS-section drawings,
let's do a CROSSword puzzle
about Mars stuff.

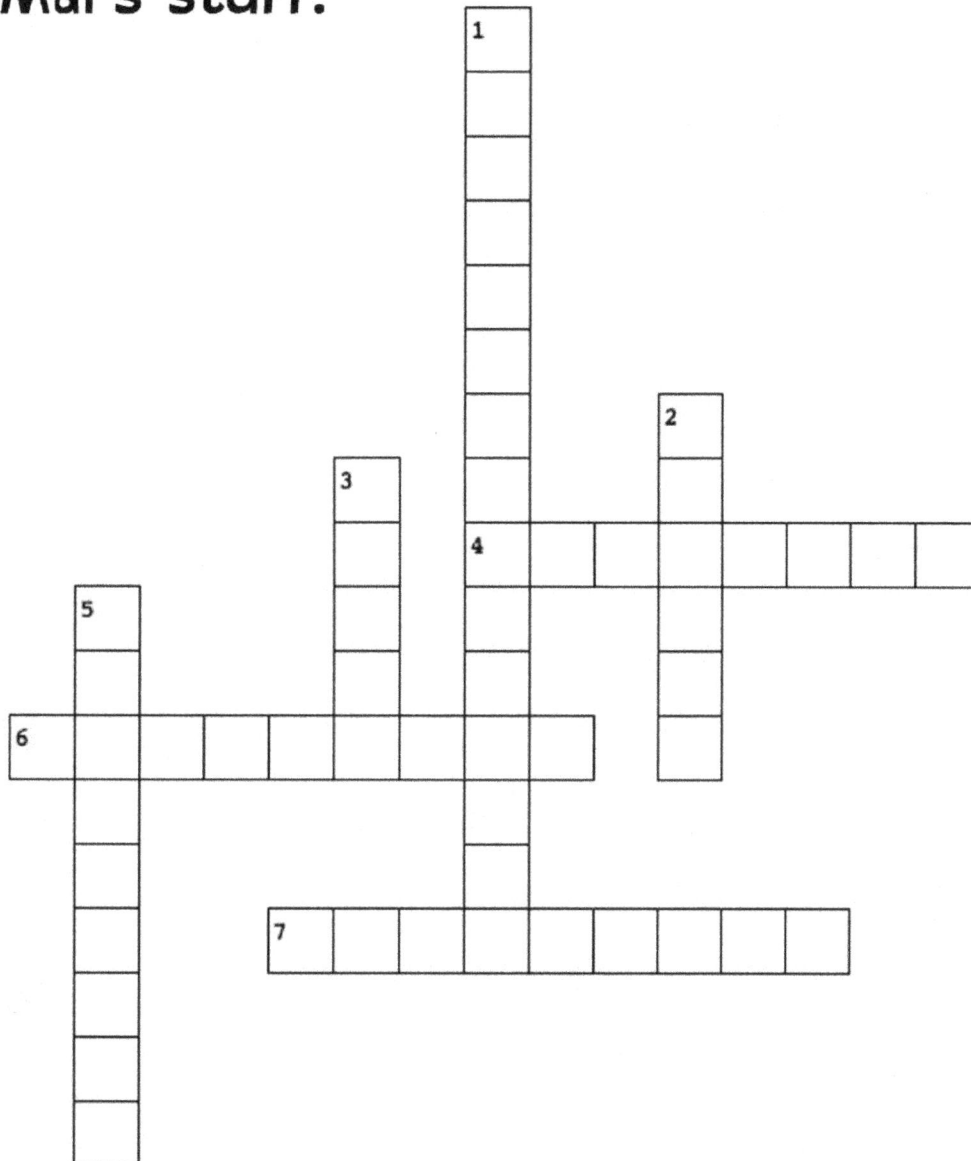

ACROSS

4. MARS DIRT
6. FIRST ROVER ON MARS
7. MARS EARTHQUAKE

DOWN

1. GRAND CANYON OF MARS
2. BIGGEST MARTIAN MOON
3. ROBOT DATA GATHERER
5. MAKES MARS RED

CROSS-SECTION DRAWINGS

Well, that was fun. Now that we kinda got an idea of what the outside looks like let's make some drawings to see what the inside looks like. I like to think of a cross-section drawing like a refrigerator. If the elevation drawing is the outside fridge door, the cross-section drawing is like opening the fridge door and looking at the stuff inside the fridge. As you know architect, we use this kind of drawing to figure out not only the structure of the building but also where things go. I wanna show off so take a look at some cross-section drawings I made for other projects.

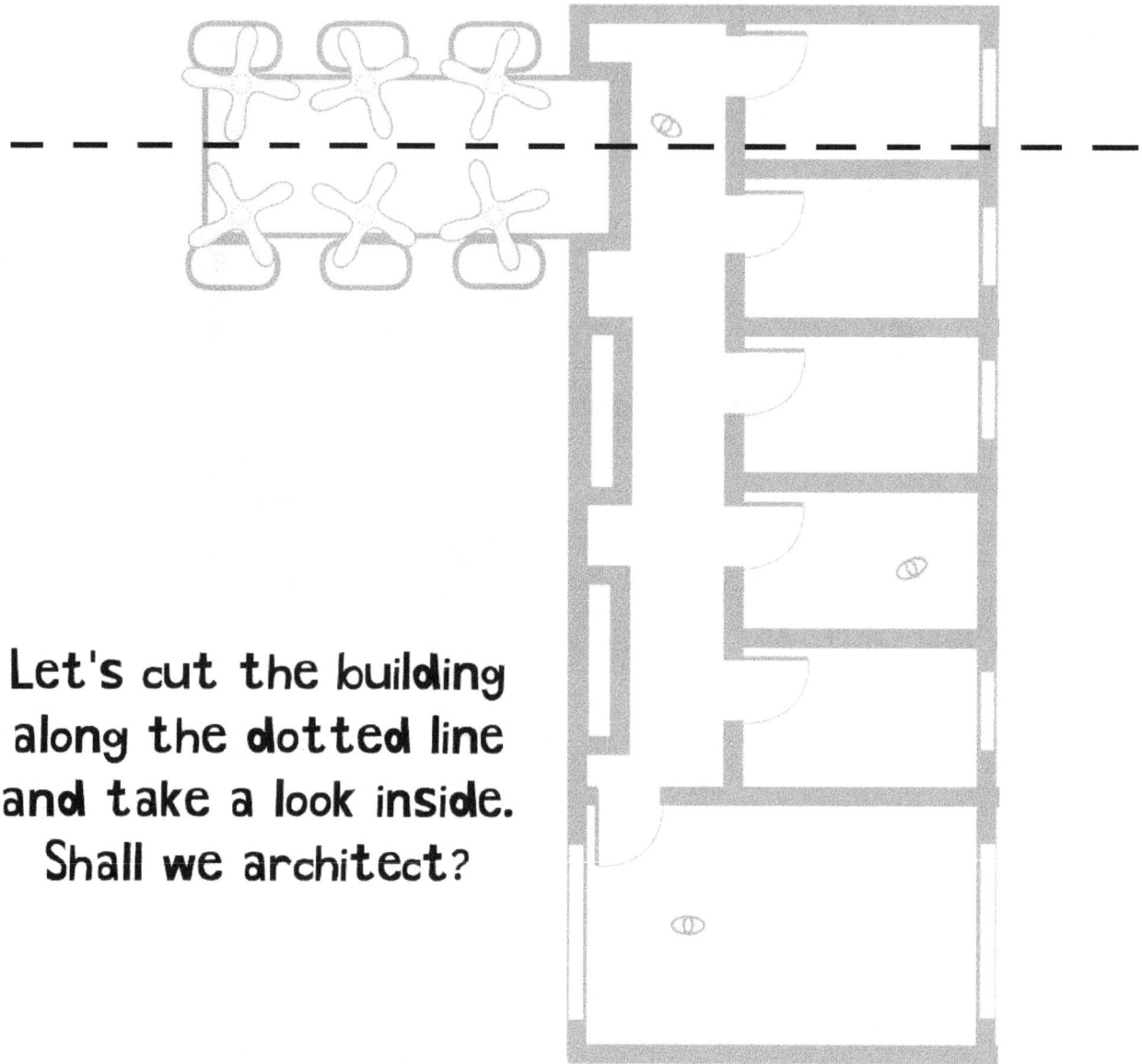

Let's cut the building
along the dotted line
and take a look inside.
Shall we architect?

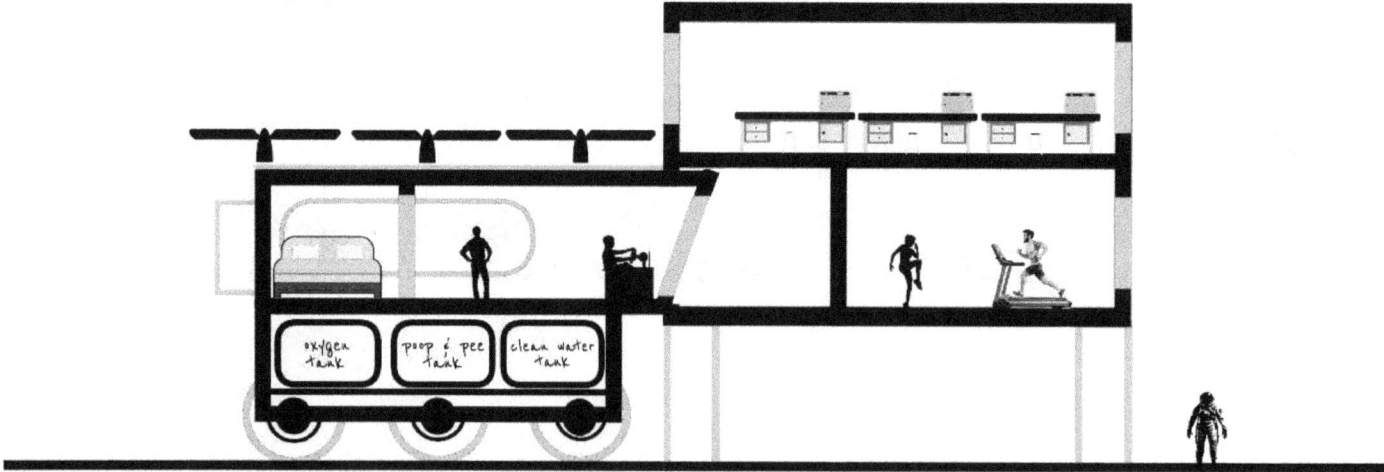

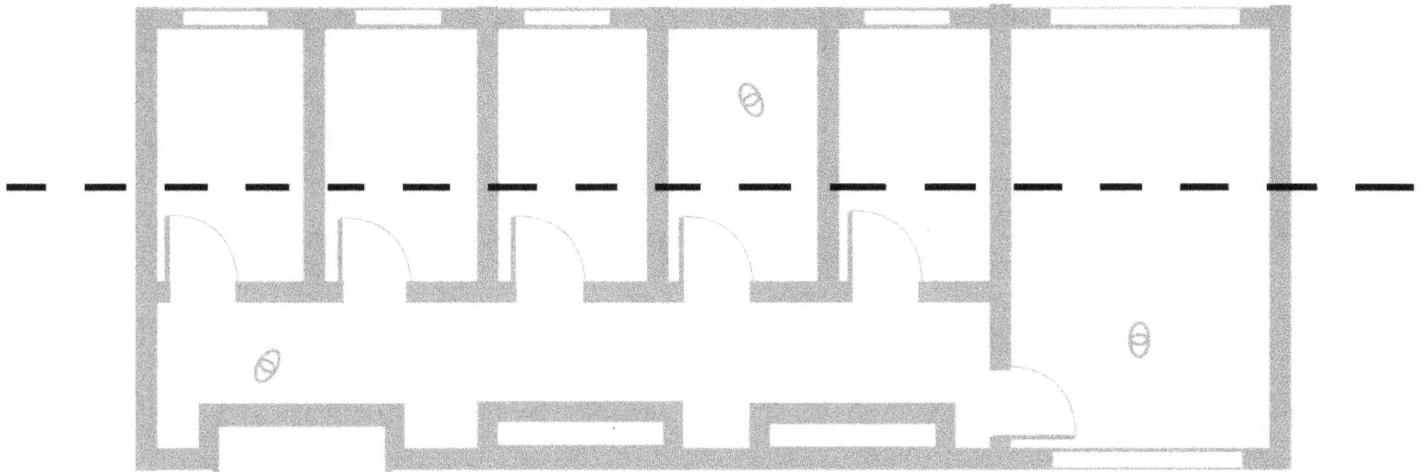

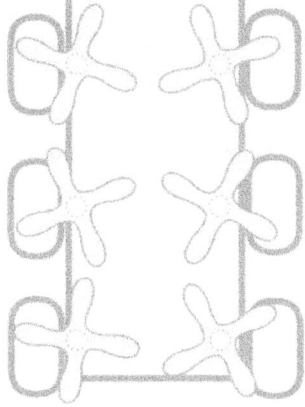

If we cut the Mars House along the dotted line, what would it look like inside? Draw it below.

PERSPECTIVE DRAWING

Well, we've now drawn the outside and the inside, and our client is starting to see our vision for this project architect. But so far we have only been drawing in 2D. Now it's time to show our client a 3D drawing of our design. So he can really start to see what it looks like. As you know architect, we can do this with a perspective drawing. But which perspective you ask? There ARE three of 'em. Well, let's see. One-point is usually for interiors, two-point is usually for exteriors and three-point perspective is usually for cities. So it looks like it's gonna be two-point. I kinda forgot how to draw a two-point perspective though. Let's take the drawing lesson on the following pages to refresh our memories.

TWO
POINT
PERSPECTIVE

refresher
lesson

1.

Draw a line.

(lightly, 'cause it's gonna be erased later)

Think of it as sky above the line.

This is the horizon line.

Land below the line.

2.

Put **2 dots** on the line.

These will be the **vanishing points.**

It's important, "cause most of the lines will connect to these two dots.

3. Let's draw some lines.

Draw a vertical line perpendicular to the horizon line.

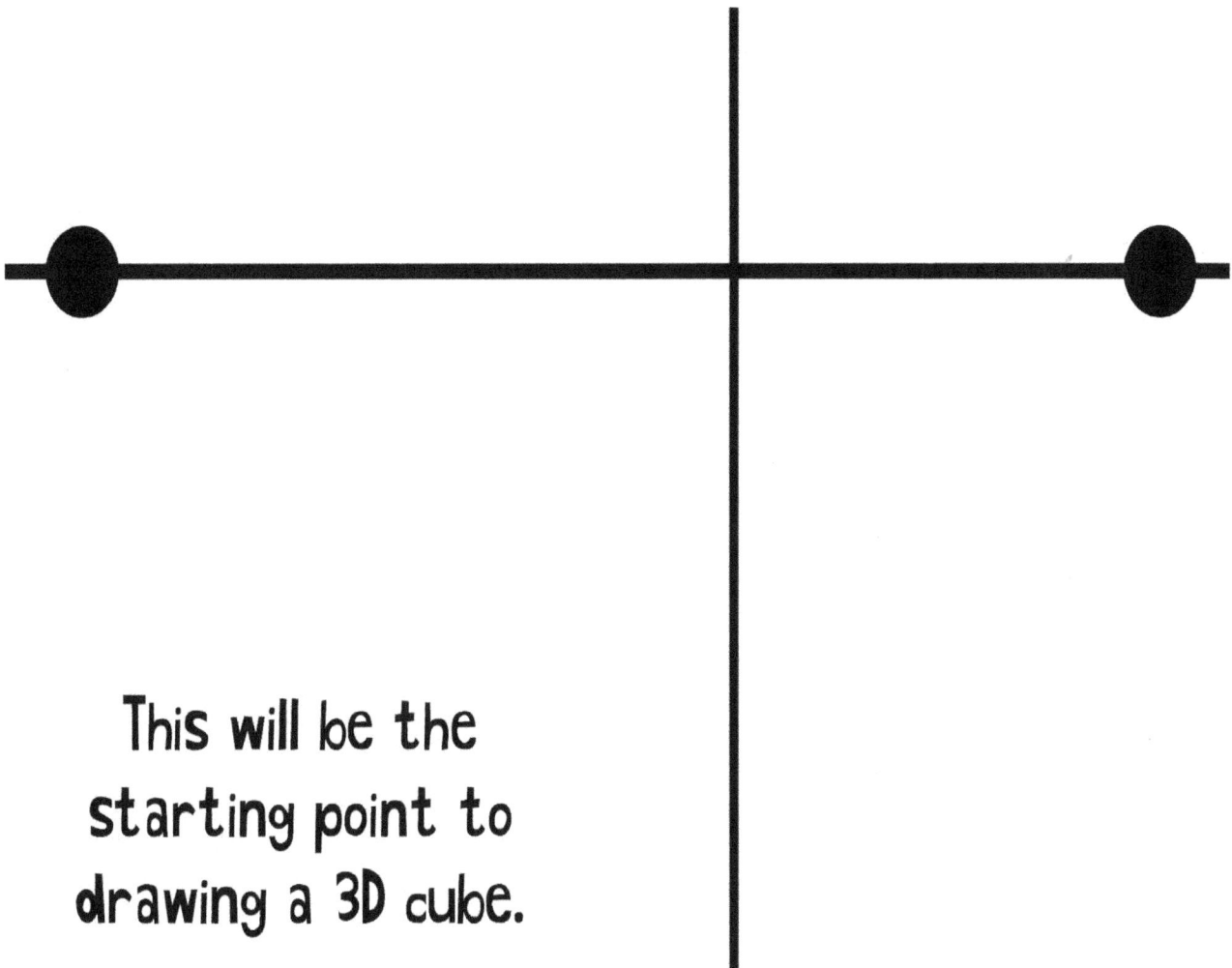

This will be the starting point to drawing a 3D cube.

4. Let's draw guidelines.

(keep 'em light to erase later)

Draw lines from the top and
bottom of your vertical line to
the two points like this.

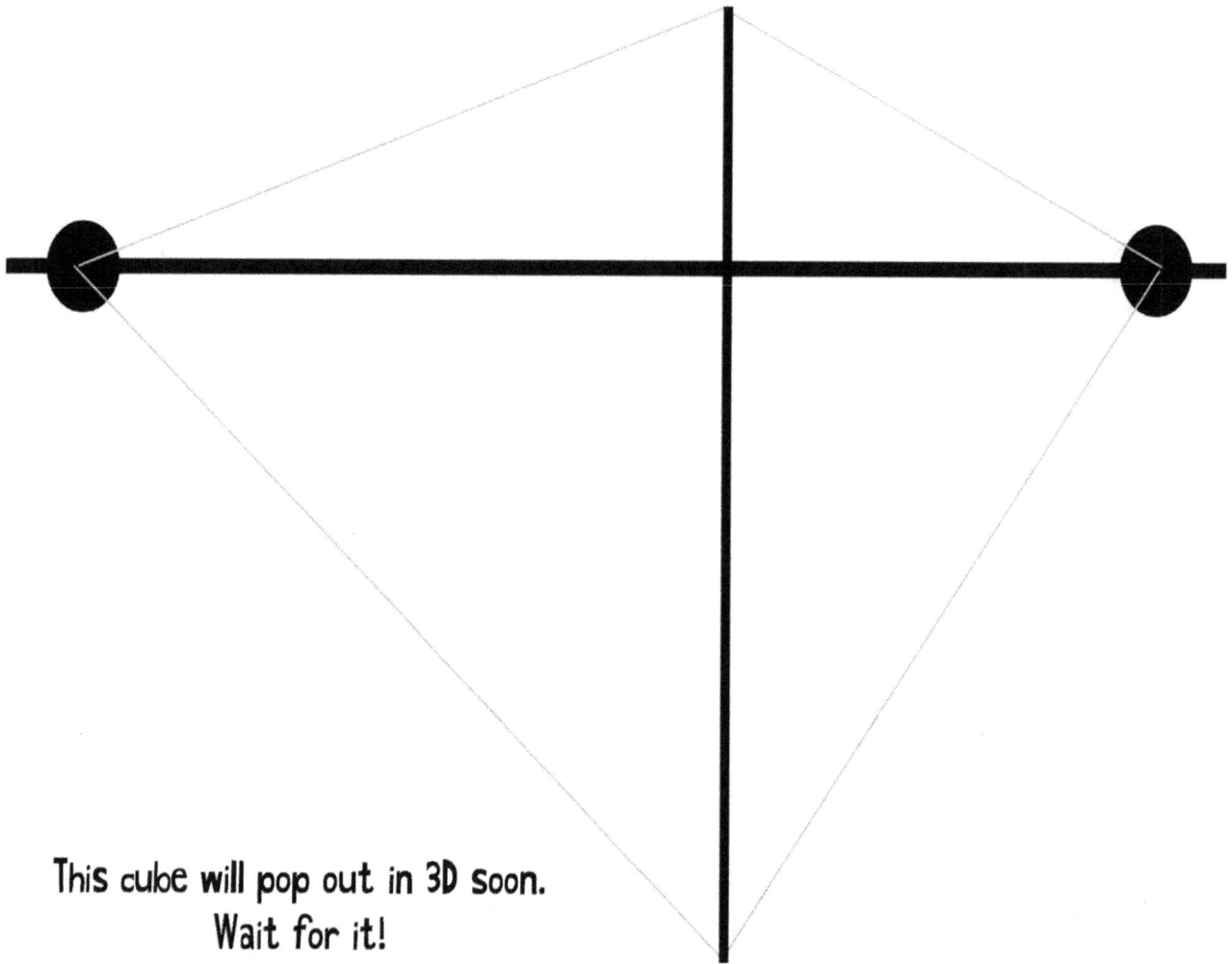

This cube will pop out in 3D soon.
Wait for it!

5. Let's draw *more* guidelines.

(keep 'em light to erase later)

Draw in the two vertical lines first.

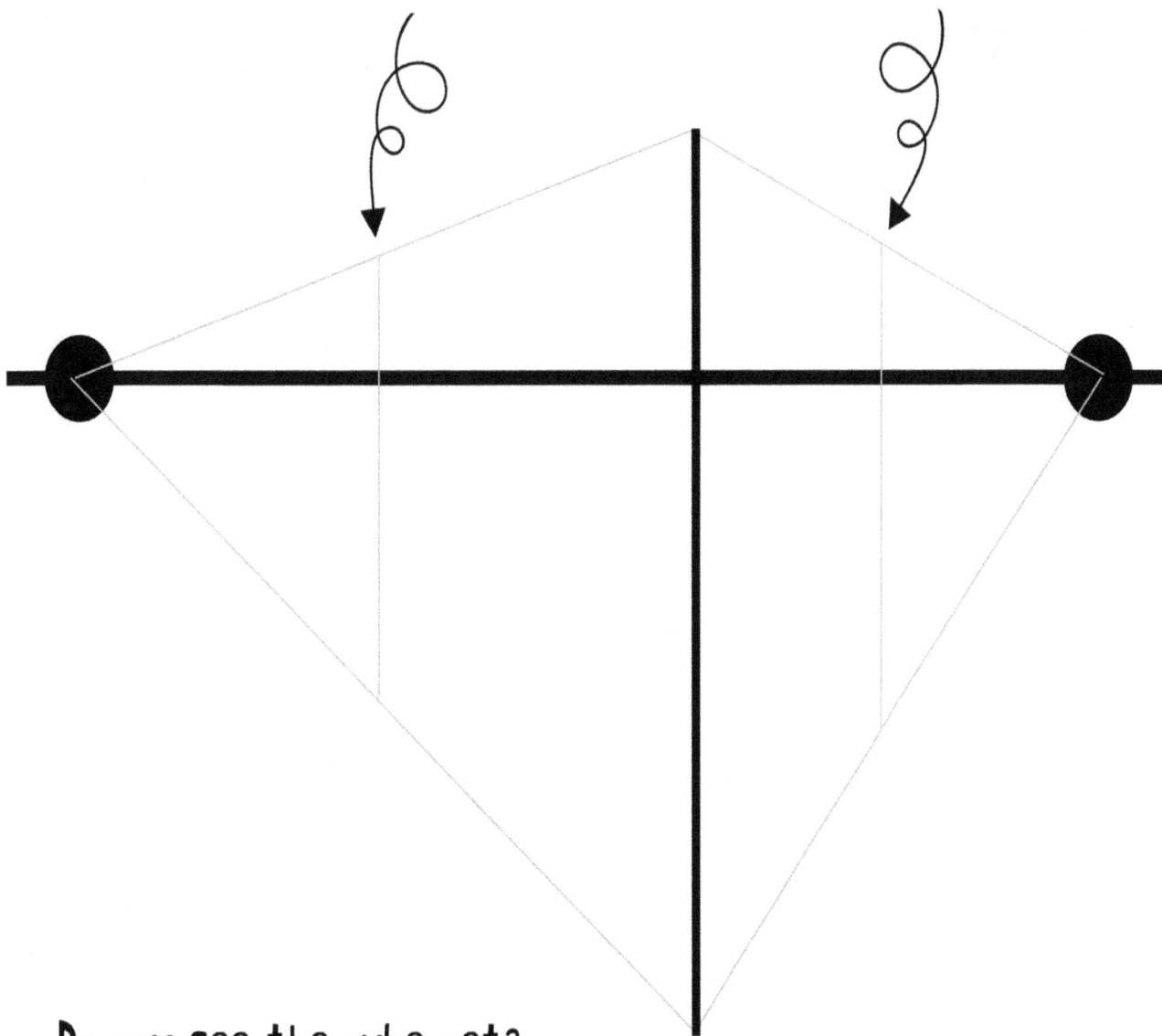

Do you see the cube yet?

6. Let's draw more guidelines.

(keep 'em light to erase later)

From the top and bottom of
those vertical lines, draw lines
to the vanishing points.

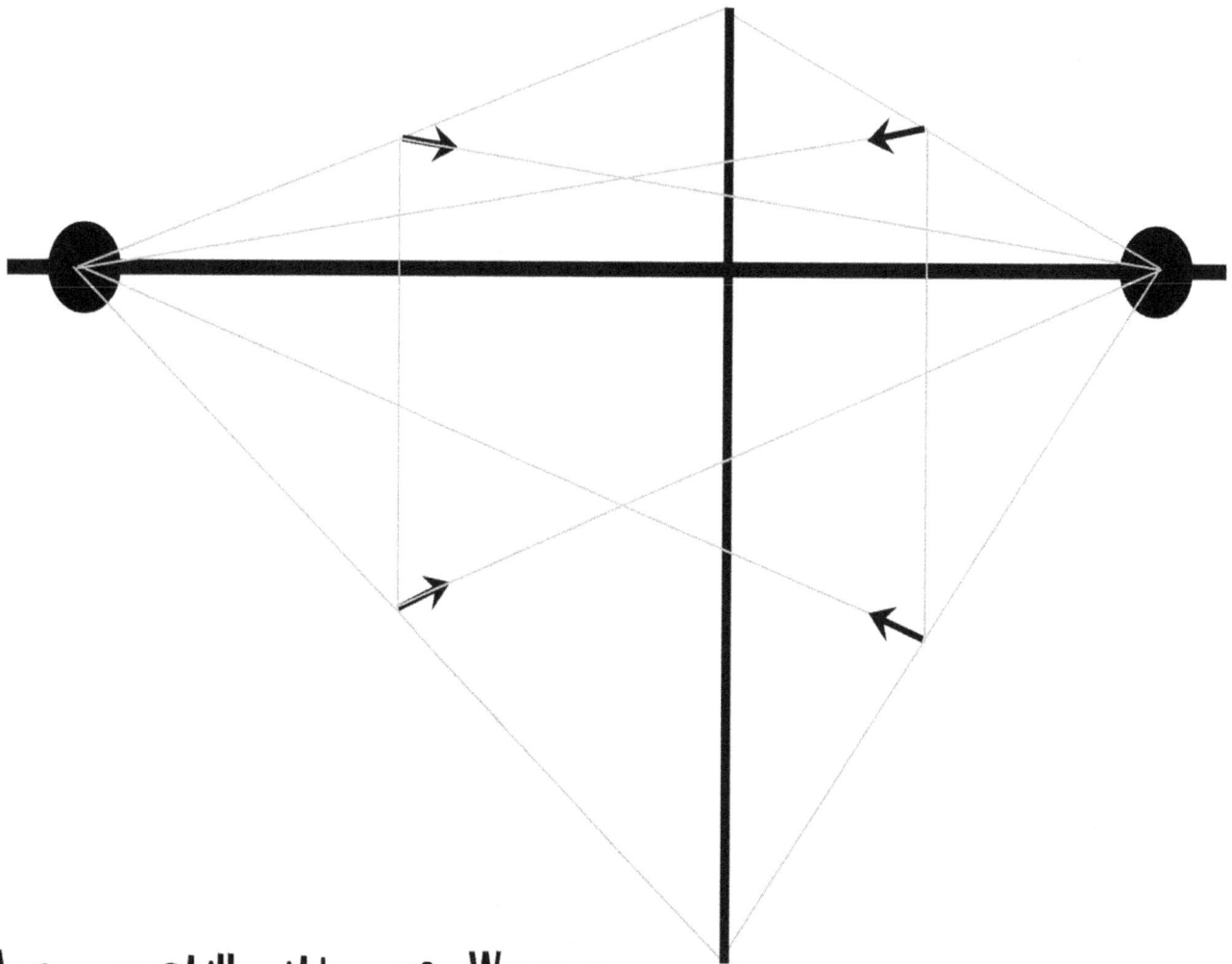

Are you still with me? We are
almost there.

7. Let's get rid of some lines.
(and make some new ones)

Now, it's time to
highlight the lines we
want to keep.

This is the **solid** cube.

8. Let's get rid of some lines.

(and make some new ones)

Now, it's time to
highlight the lines we
want to keep.

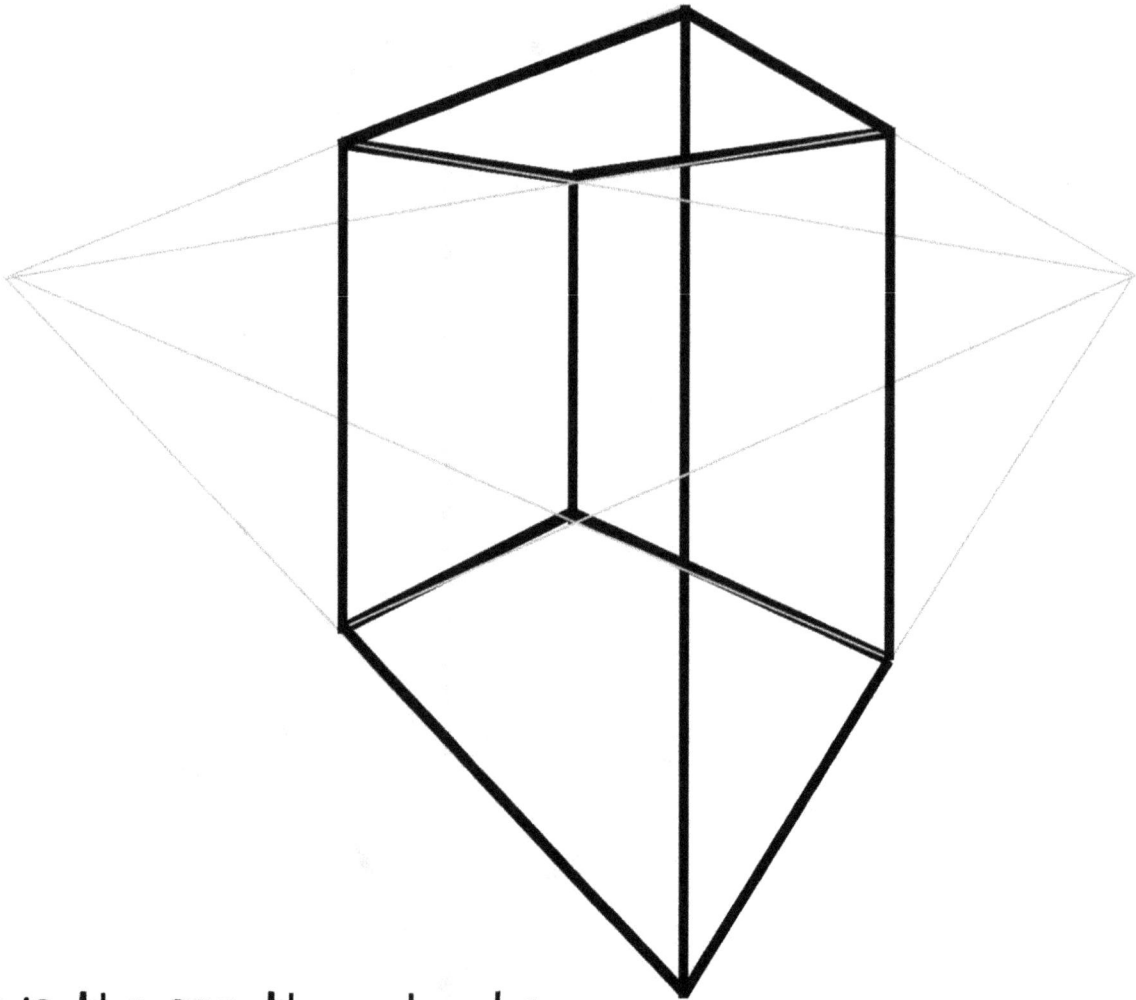

This is the see-through cube.

9.

Erase the guidelines.

VOILA! There you have it!!!

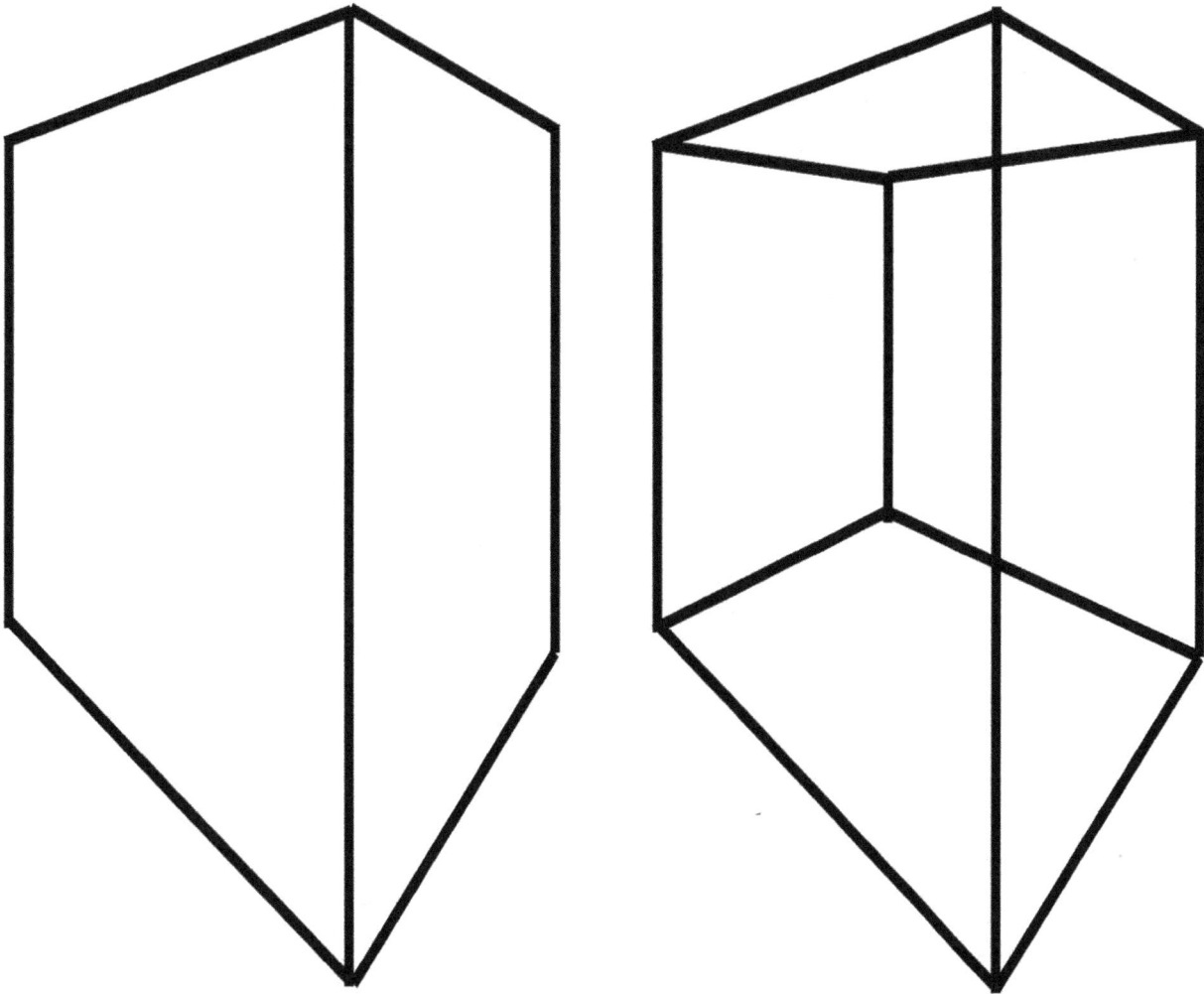

Solid or see-though. It's entirely up to you.

Give it a try here!

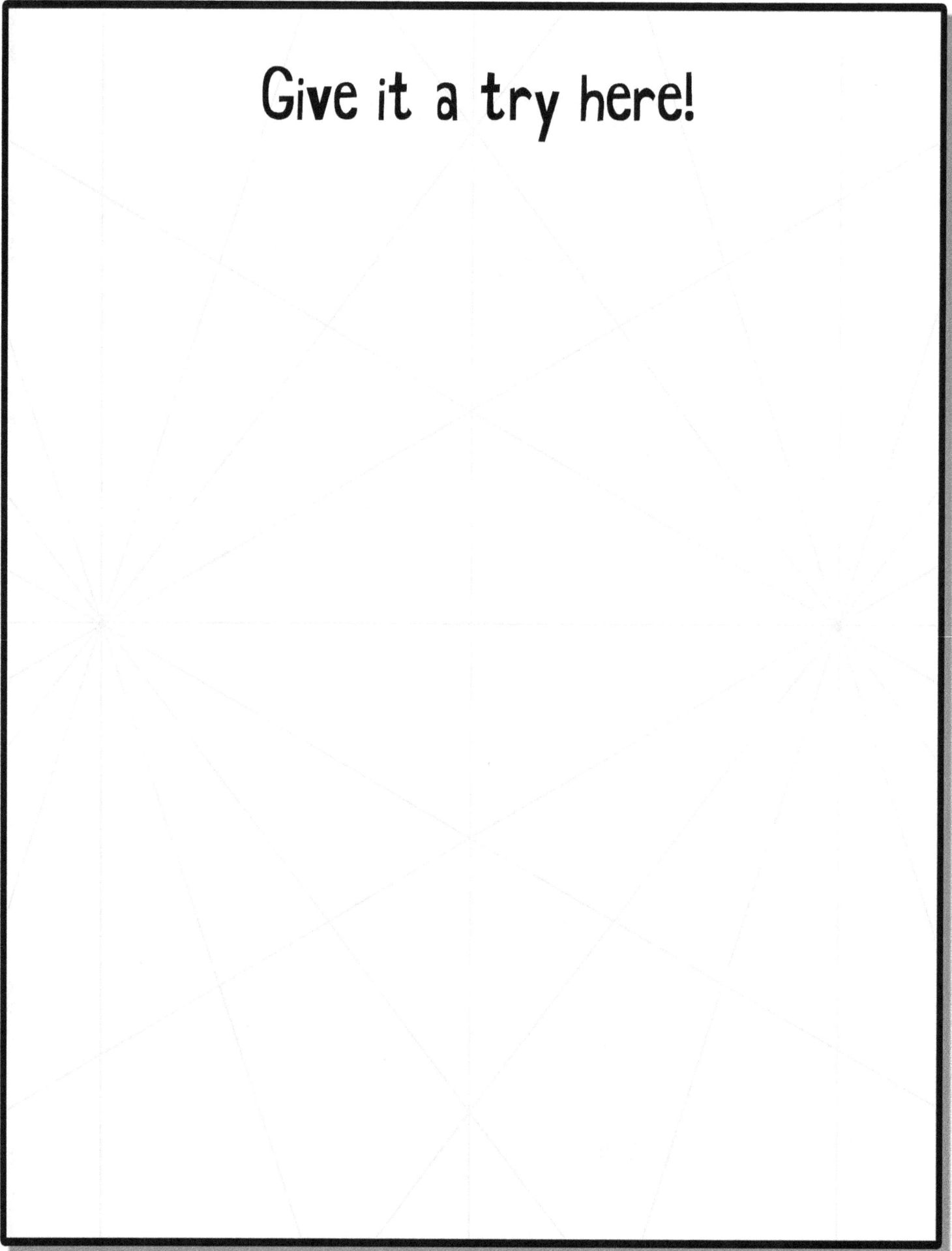

Give it a try here!

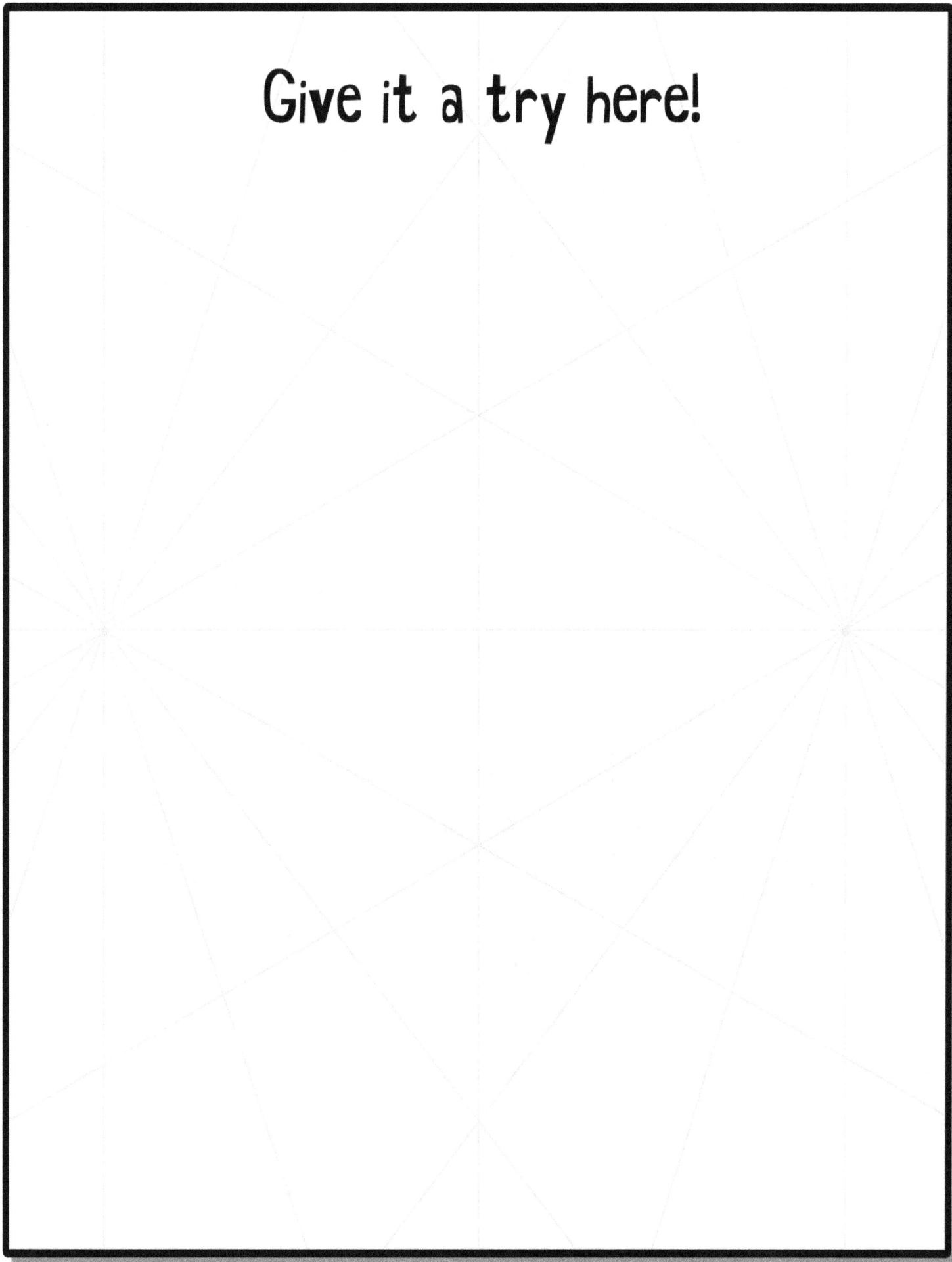

Hey architect! Let's start the two-point perspective of the Mars House.

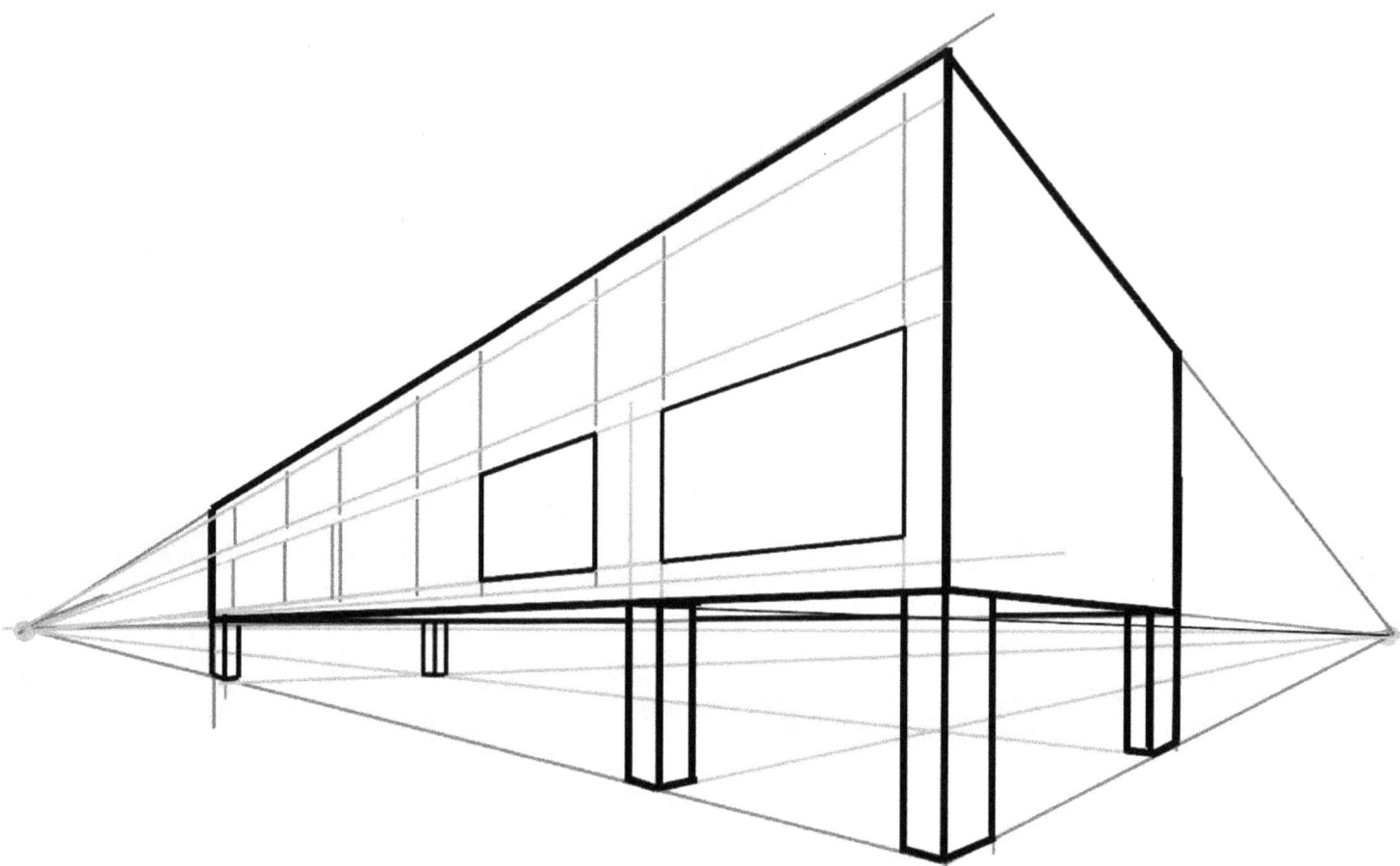

Add more details to show windows and textures.

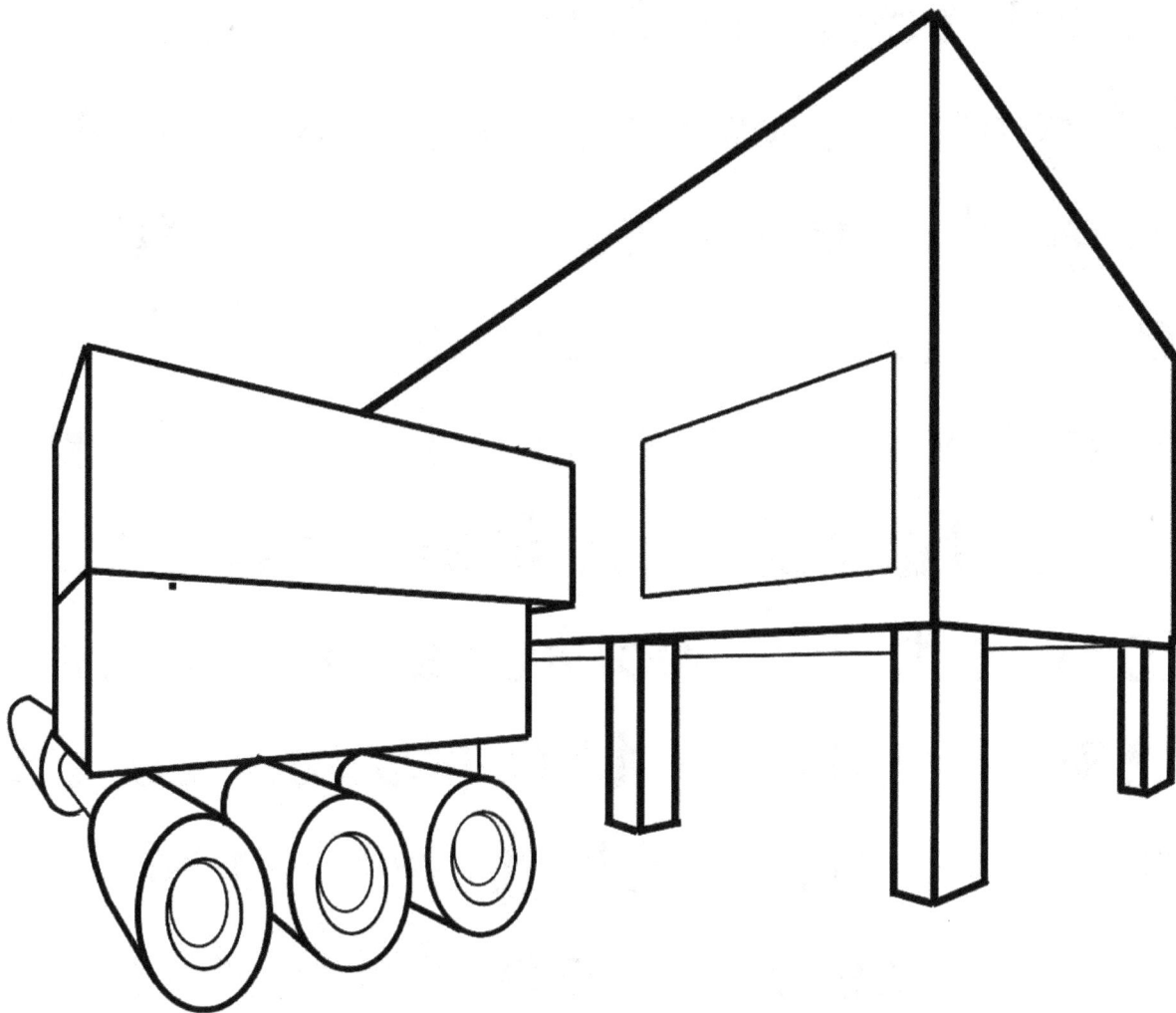

Remember: Use the two gray dots on the sides to get the angles right.

THE 3D MODEL

So architect, before THE SPACE AGENCY gives the green light on our design they want to see a 3D model of this Mars House. If they approve then the robots can start building THE PORT on Mars and at the same time, workers on Earth can start building the MODUs to be placed in the rocket with the astronauts who can drive the MODUs to where THE PORT will be built and waiting for docking. So, I have supplied you with the model pieces and directions on the following pages. Let's get to it!!!

INSTRUCTIONS

The first thing you need to do architect is find something to use as the base. Something like a piece of thick paper or cardboard about the size of this book. If necessary you can cut off and use the back cover of this book.

thick paper or cardboard

Glue the floor plan guide to the cardboard or thick paper base.

NOTE: If you would like to color the surface of Mars red, now is a good time to do it!!!

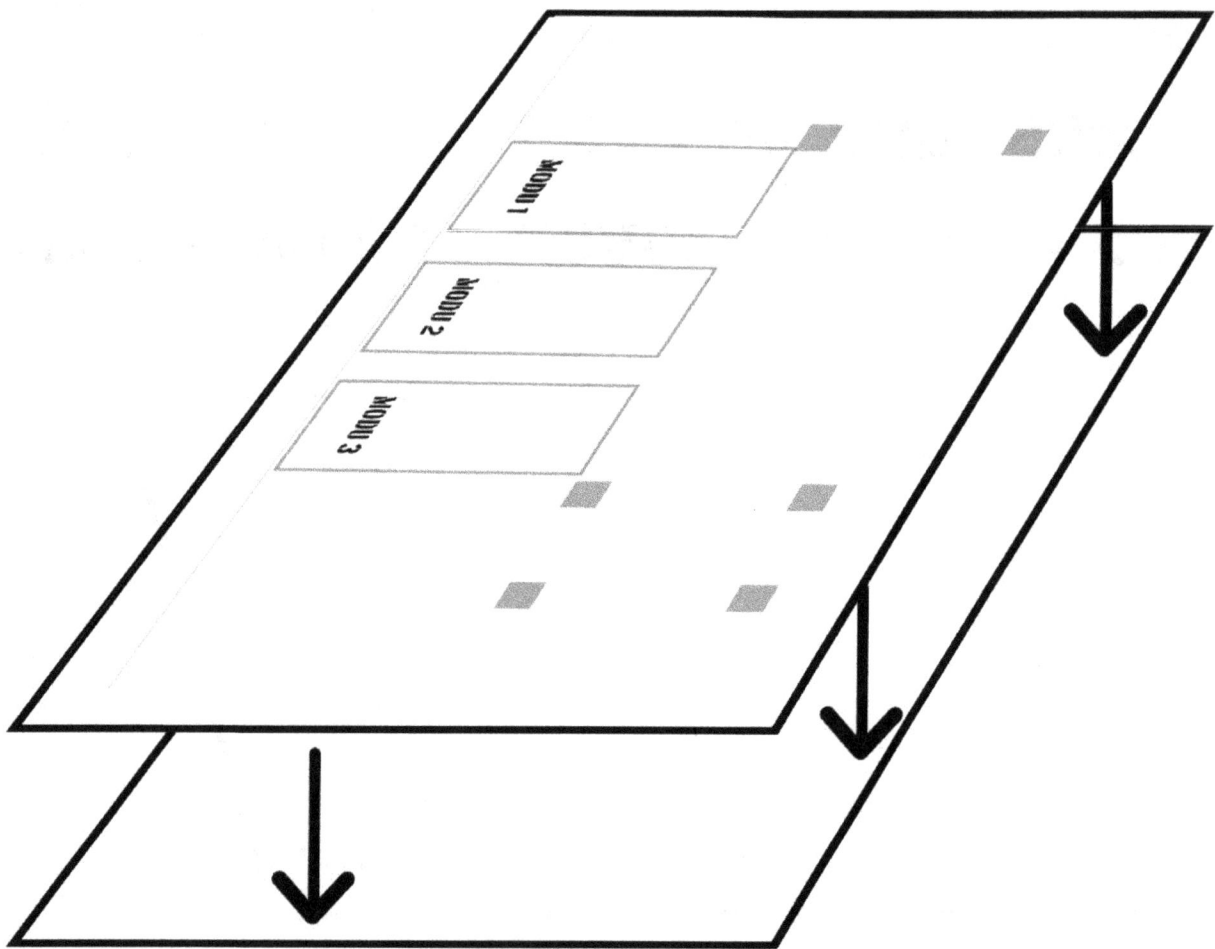

MODU 1

MODU 2

MODU 3

GLUE THIS SIDE TO THE BASE

(bottom)

1. Cut out the pieces and fold them like this.

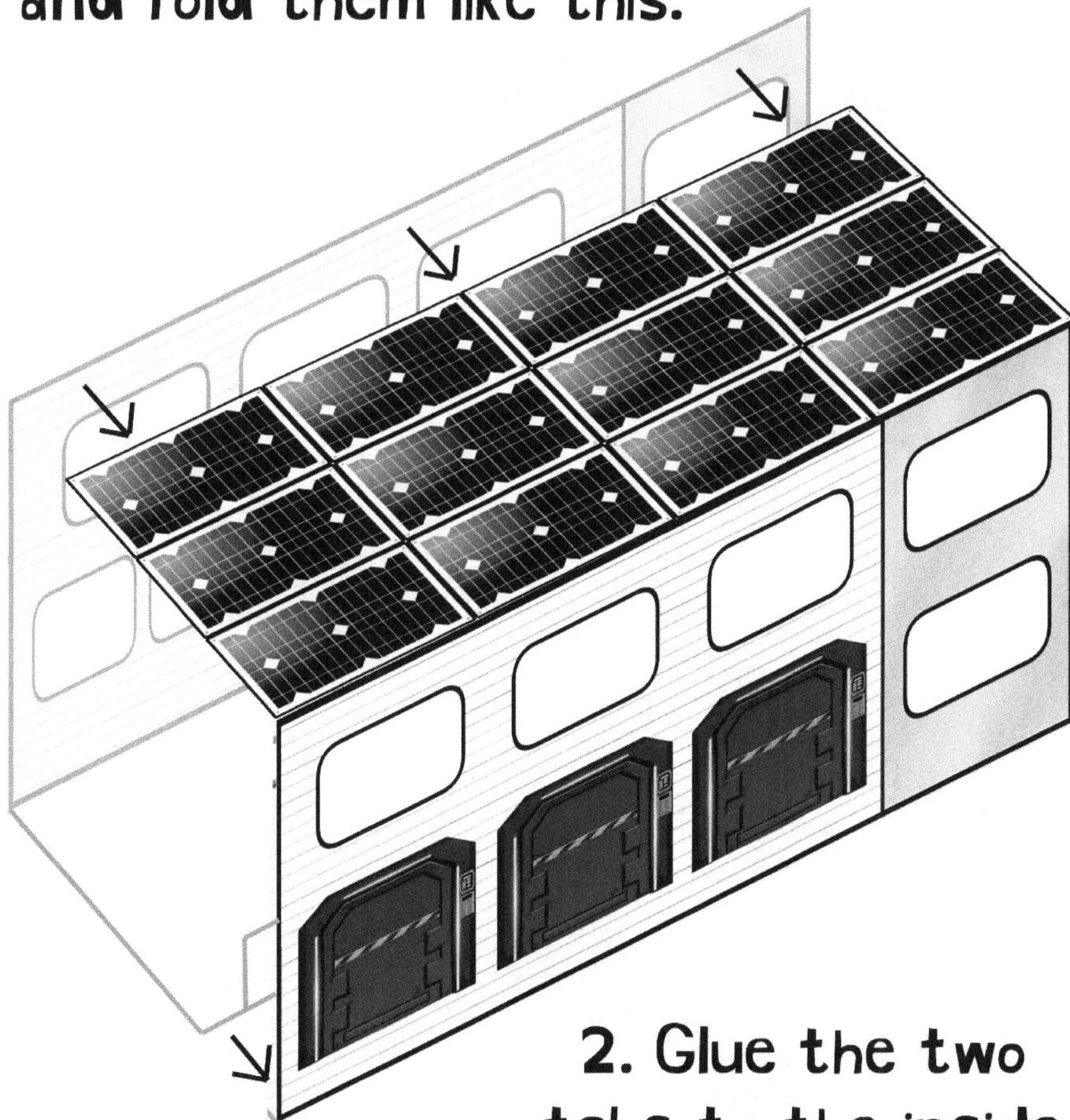

2. Glue the two tabs to the inside to make a box shape.

3. Cut out, fold, and glue the columns like this.

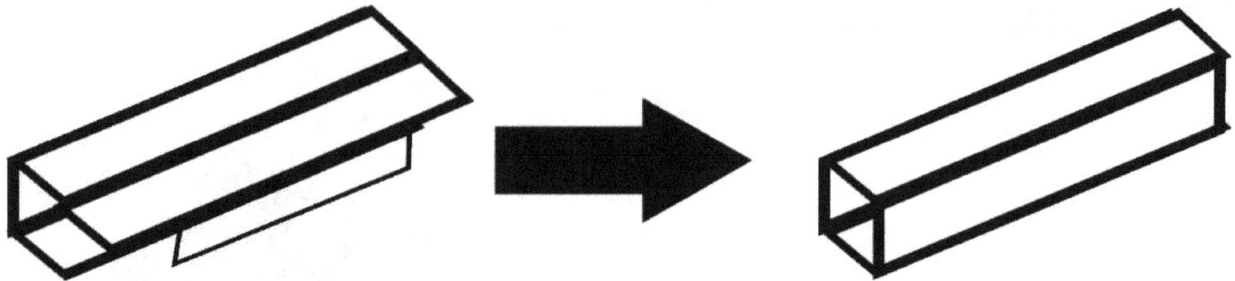

4. Cut out the side walls and glue the tabs to the inside.

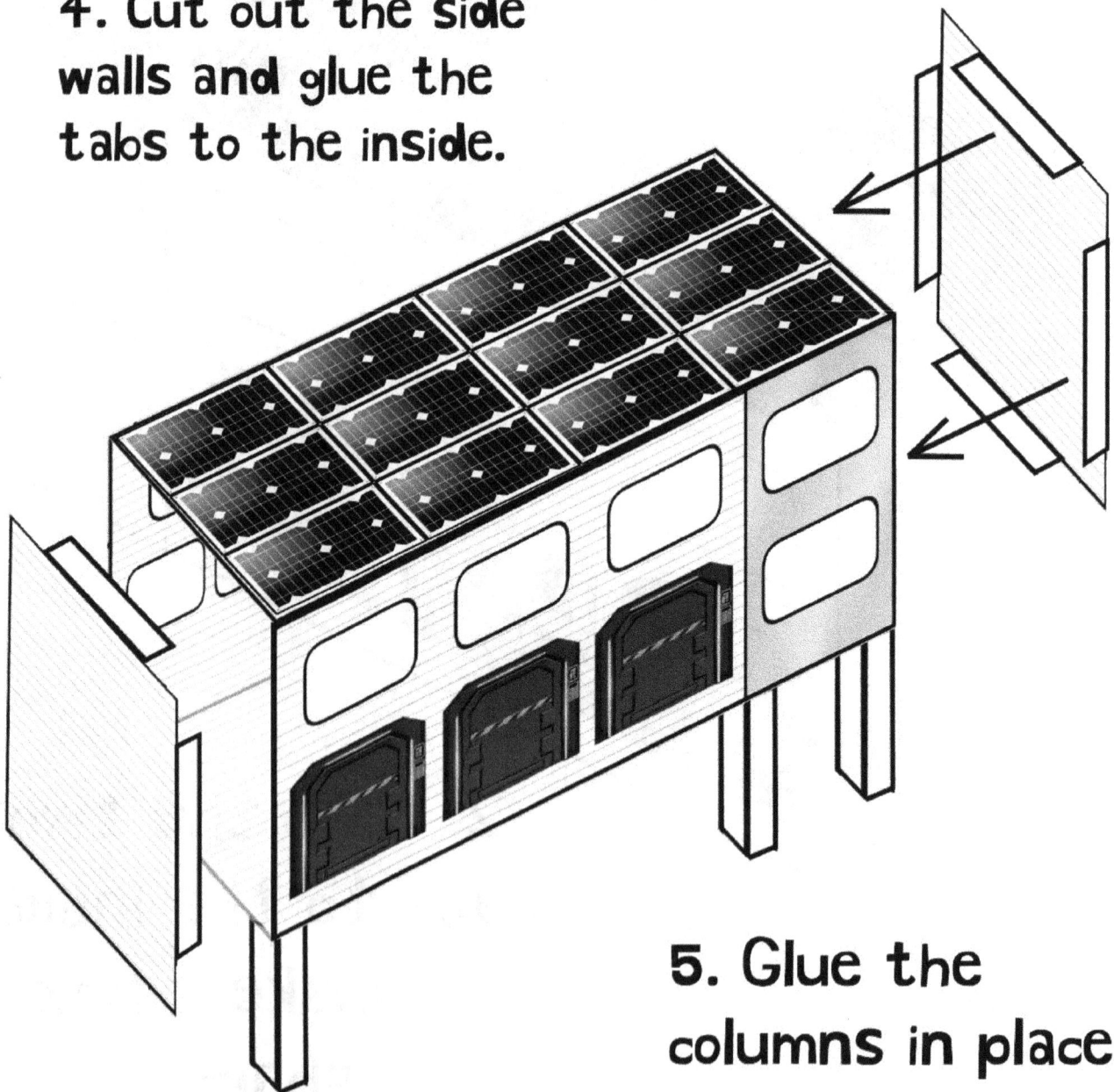

5. Glue the columns in place.

Front and Roof of The Port

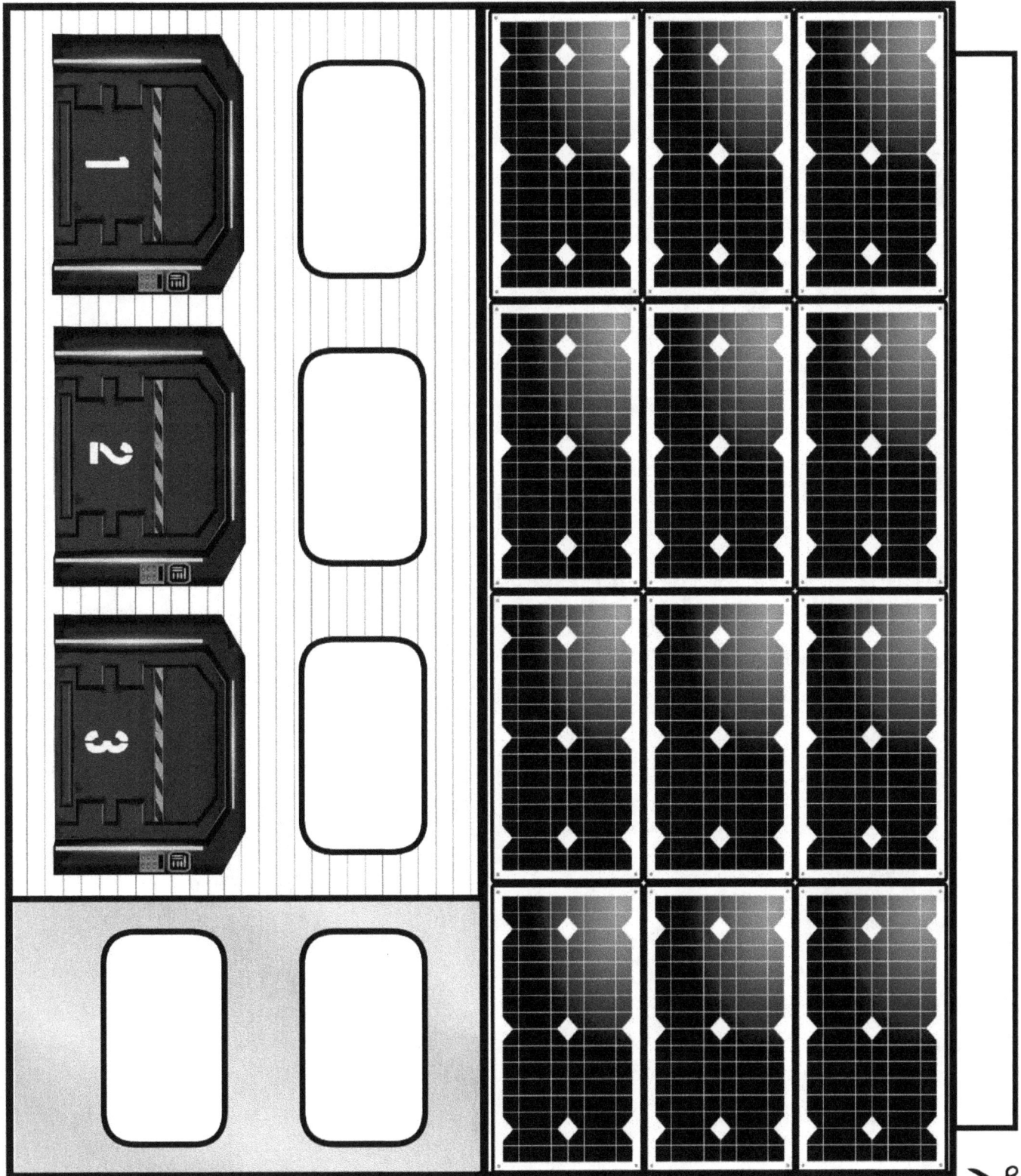

NOTE: The walls/roof are made with layers of red regolith so if you wanna color them, now is a good time!!!

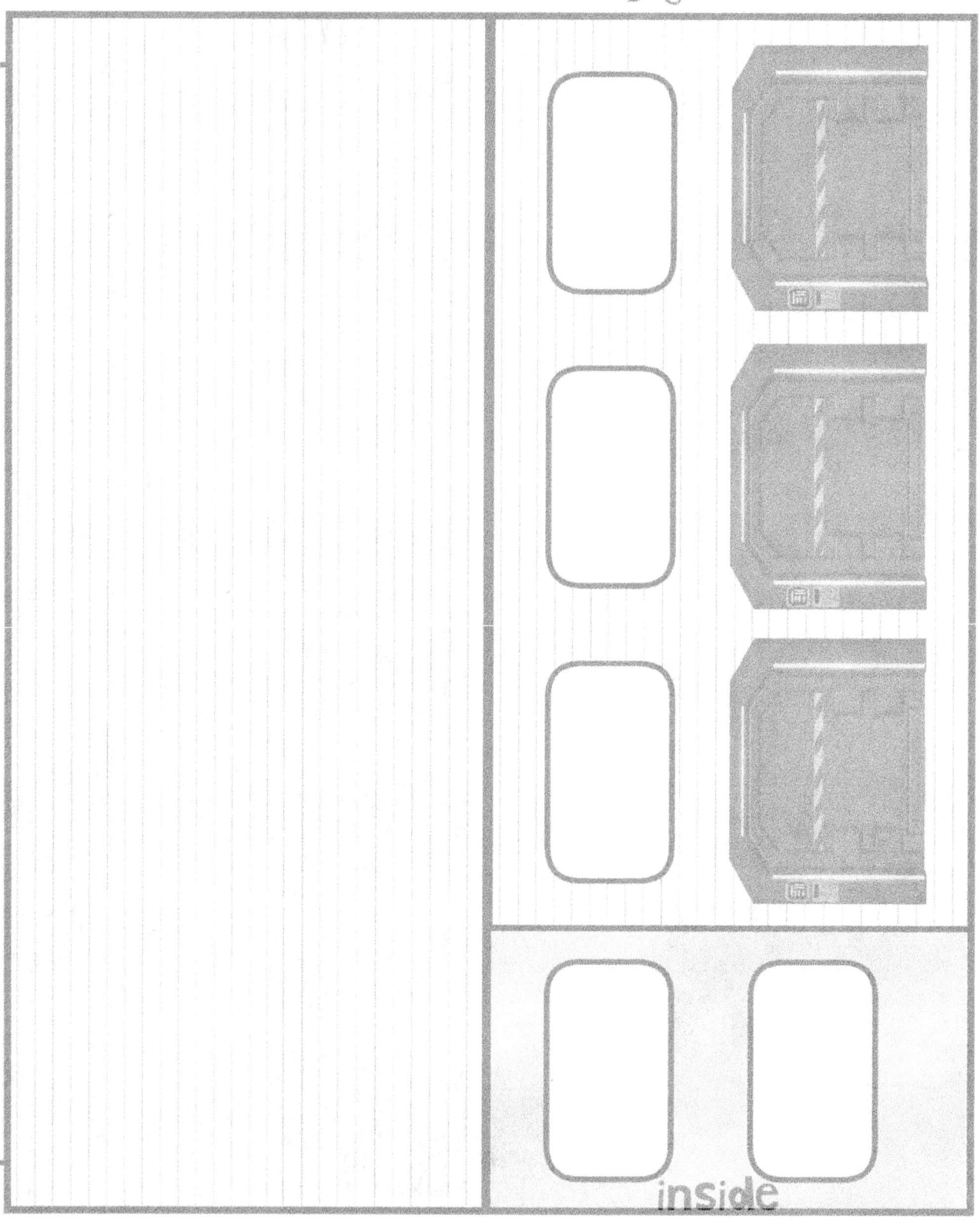

inside

Back and Underside of The Port

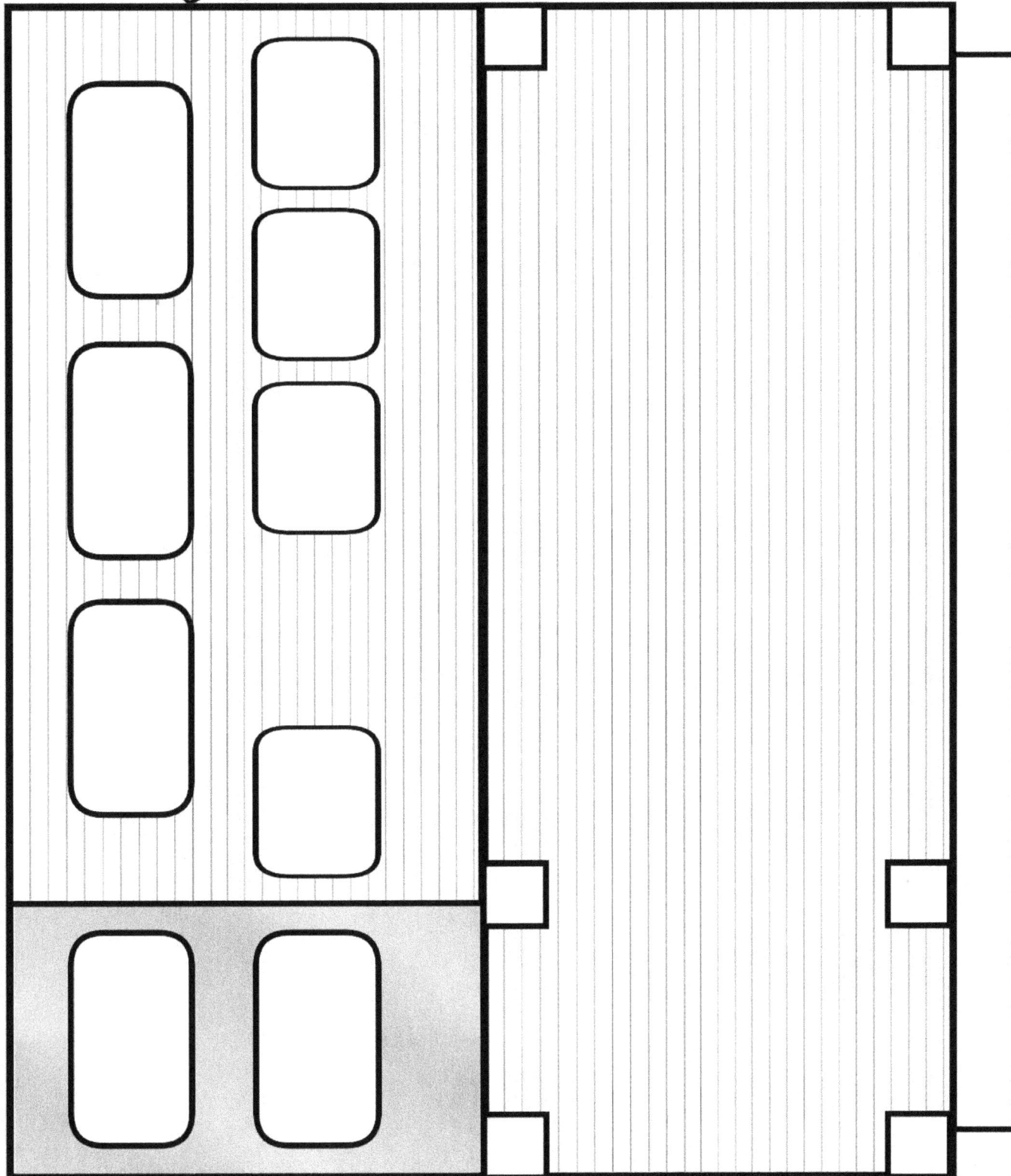

NOTE: The walls/underside are made with layers of red regolith so if you wanna color them, now is a good time!!!

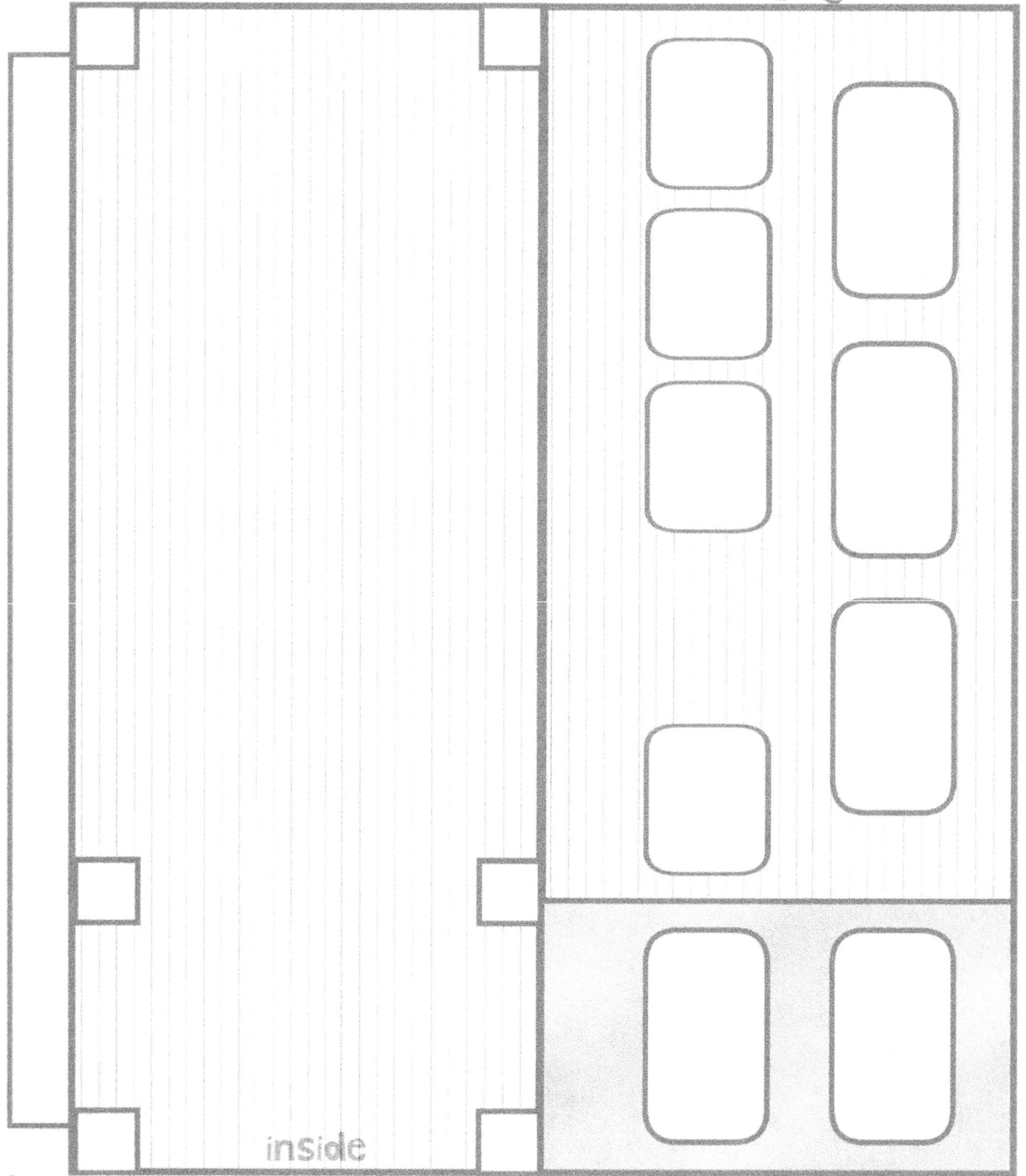

inside

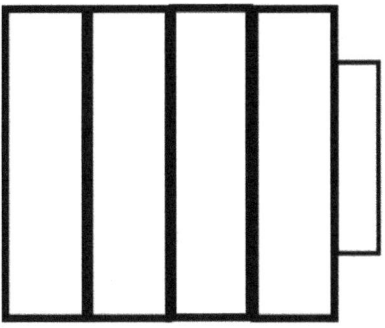

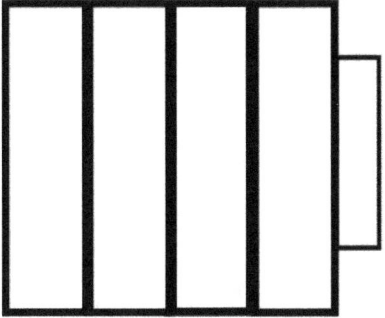

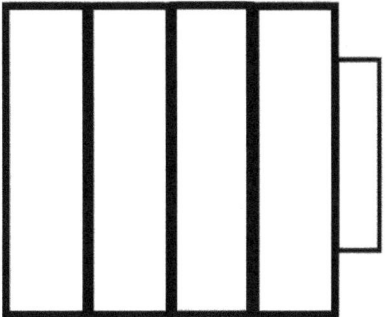

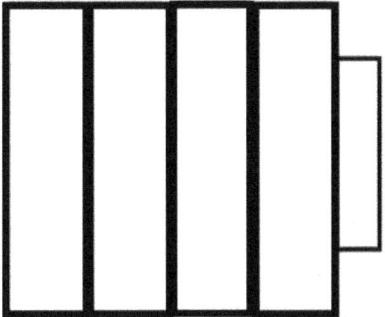

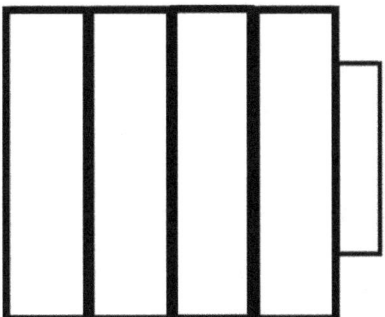

columns

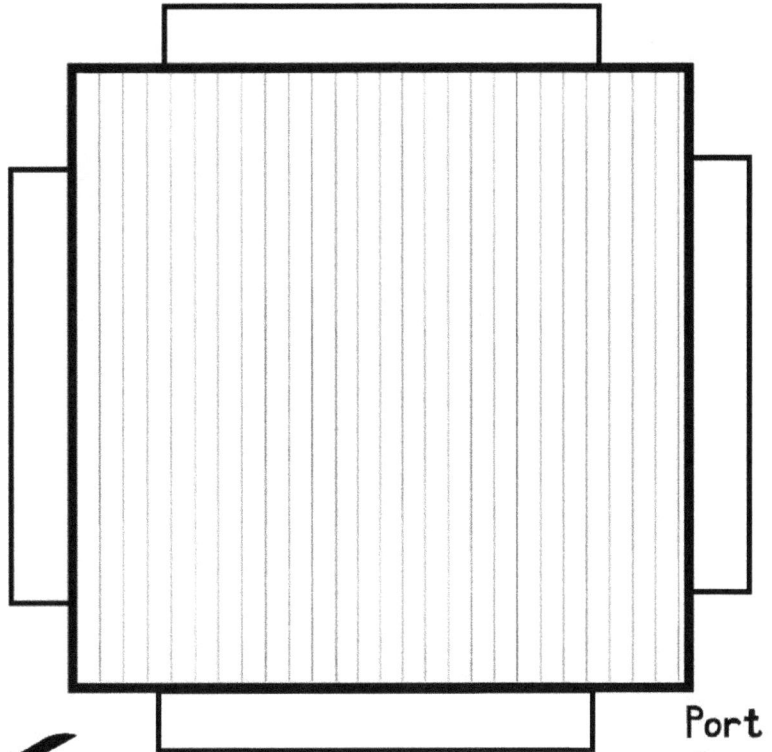

Port
Side
Walls

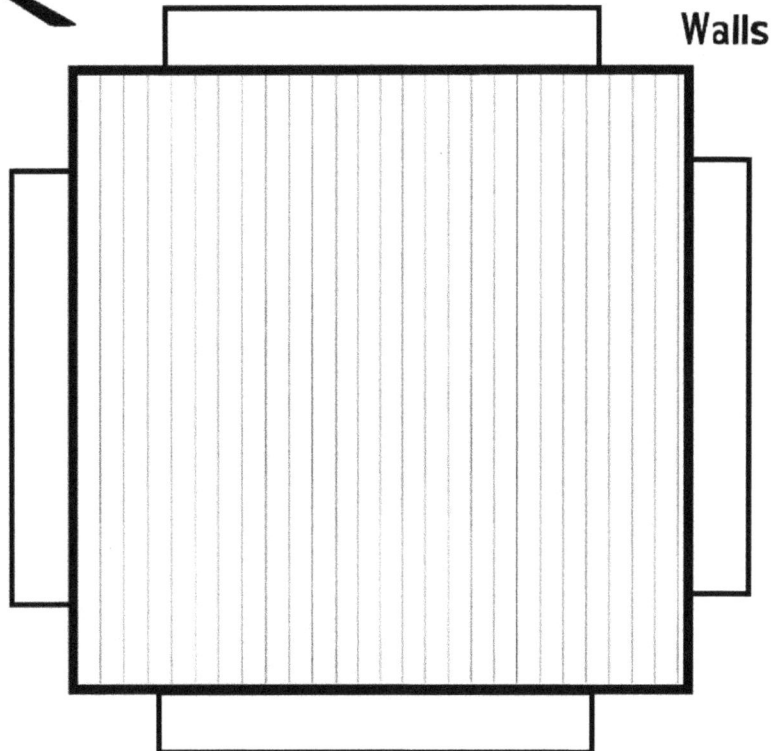

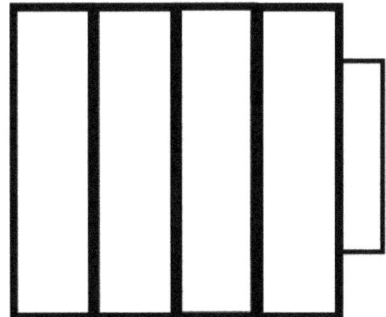

inside top

inside top

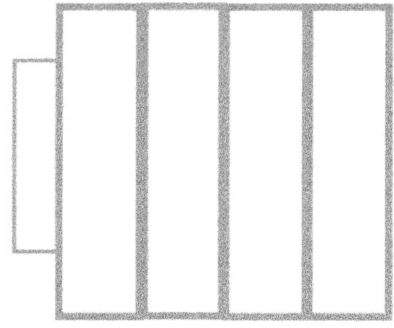

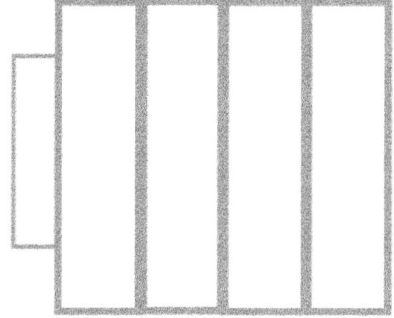

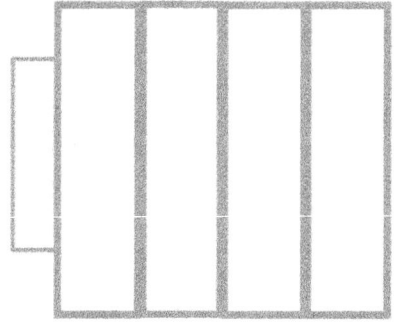

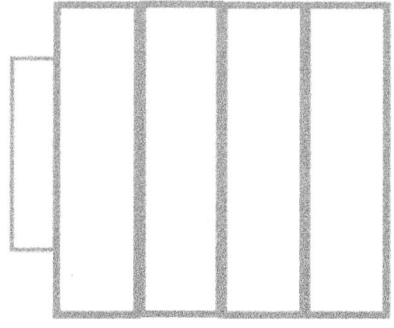

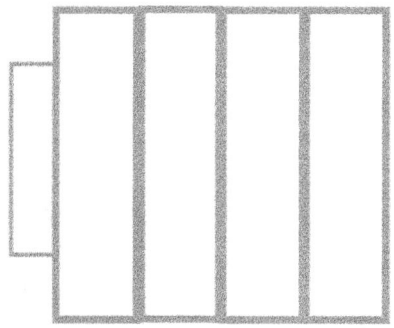

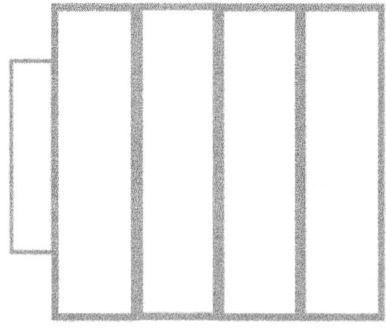

columns

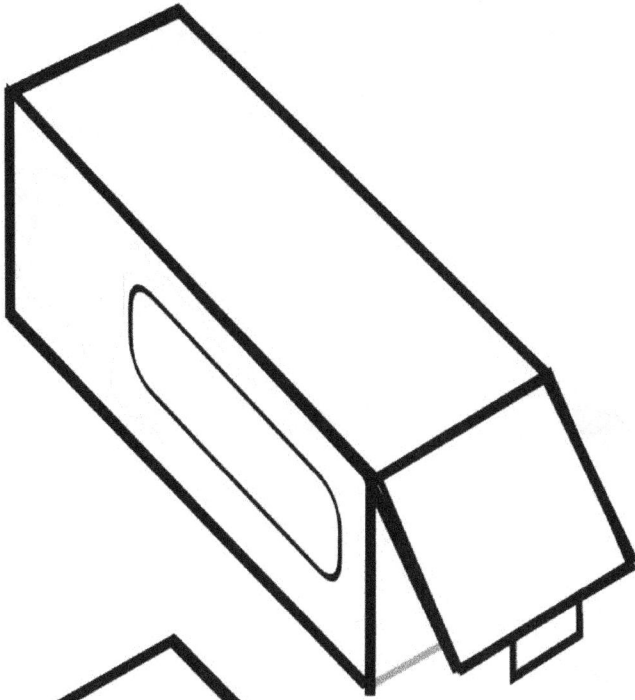

1. Cut out, fold, and glue the top section of MODU 1 into a box shape.

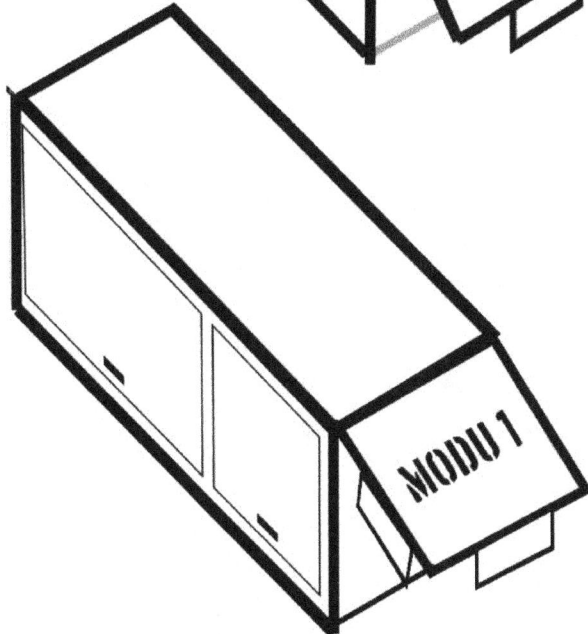

2. Cut out, fold, and glue the bottom section of MODU 1 into a box shape.

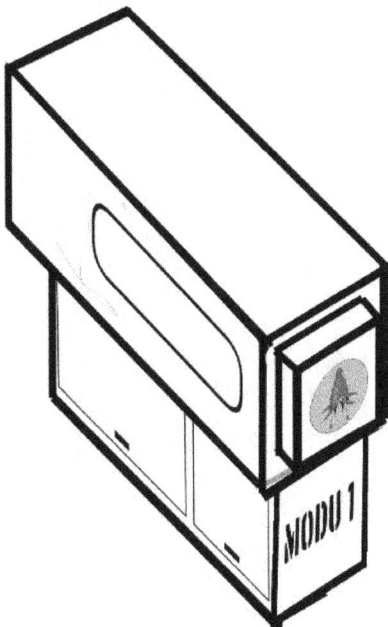

3. Glue together. Cut out, fold, and glue the battery pack.

1. Cut out the axles and use a pencil to roll them. Then using the center hole of the wheel as a guide, glue the axles into a tube shape.

2. Flip the MODU over and glue the axles on the grey lines. Centering them as best you can!

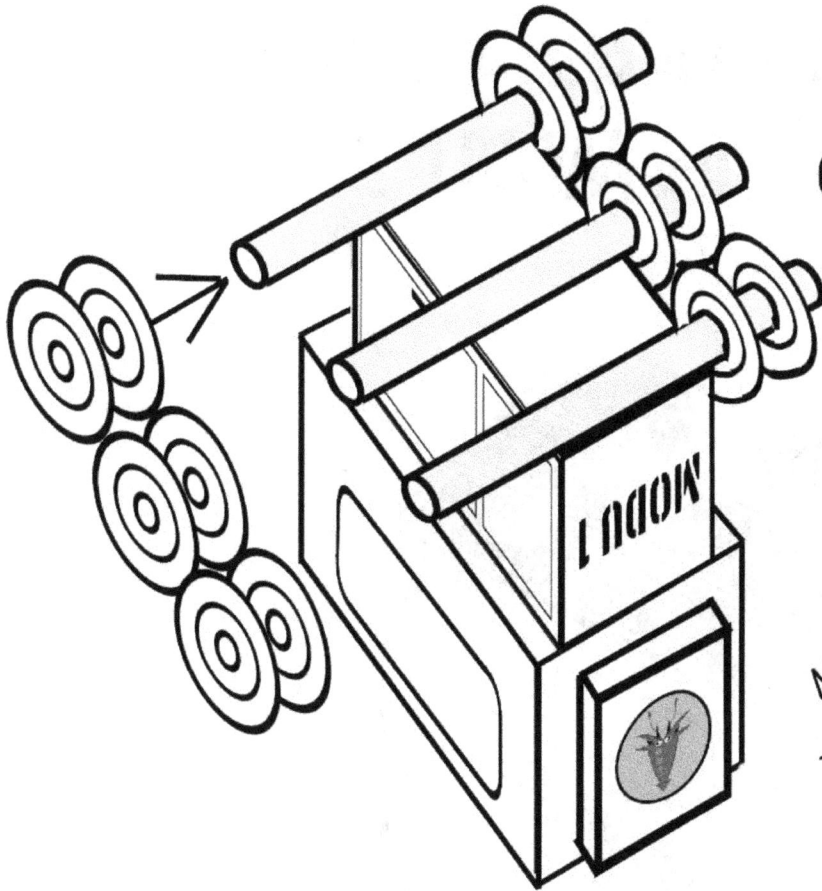

3. Cut out the wheels. Glue two wheels on each side of the axle.

NOTE: Make the width between the two wheels less than the width of the tire treads.

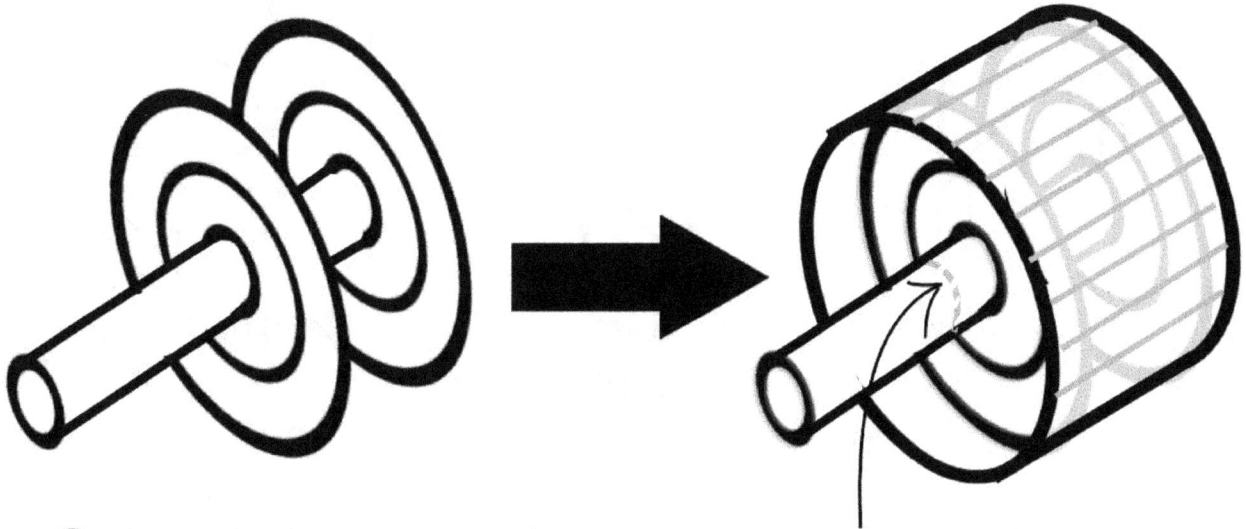

4. Cut out tire treads and wrap and glue them around the two wheels.

5. Cut off end of axles to use as propeller stands.

6. Repeat the building process to assemble MODU 3.

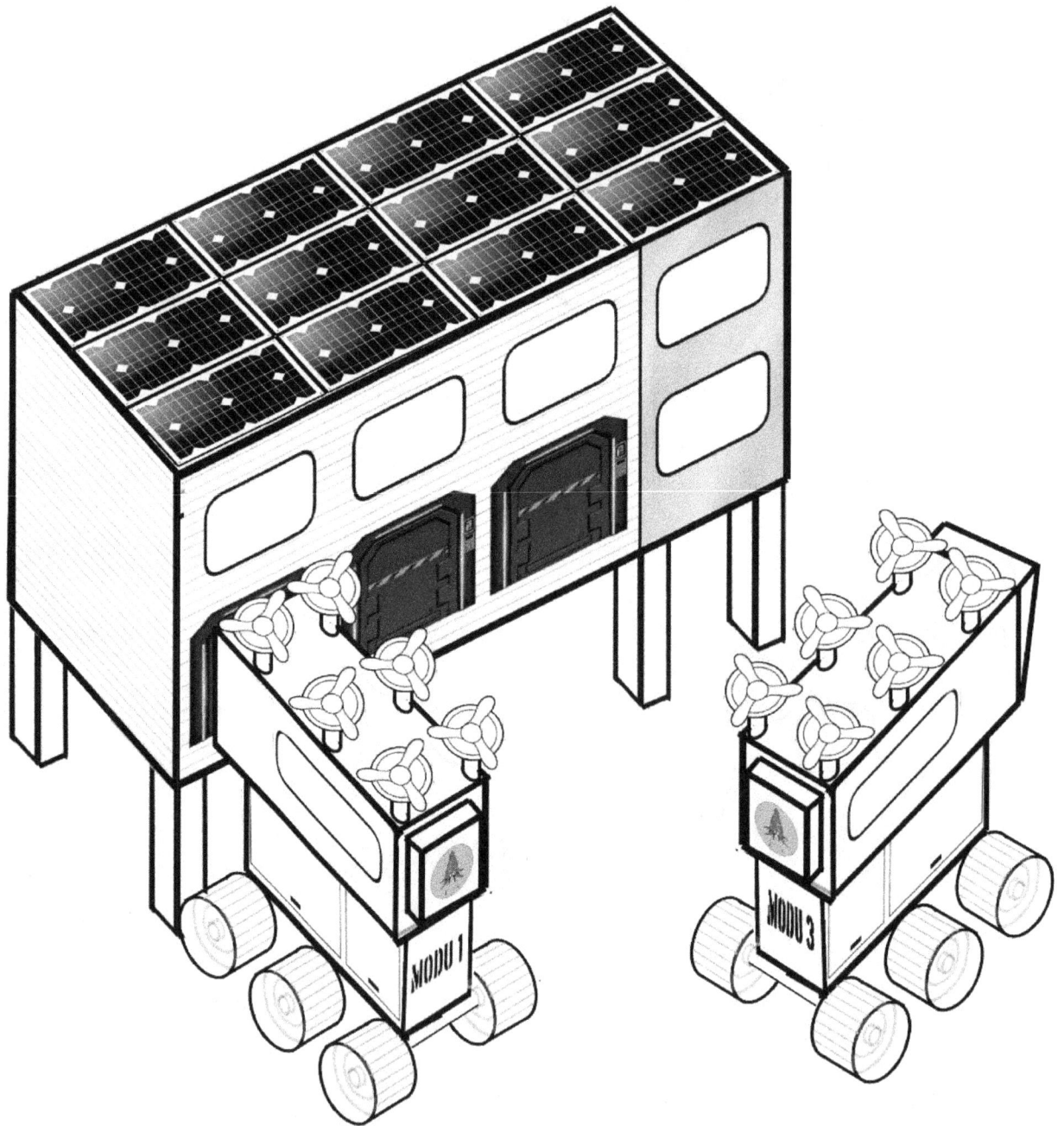

7. Glue MODU 1 to the docking station of THE PORT.
Leave MODU 3 detached.

Top Section of MODU 1

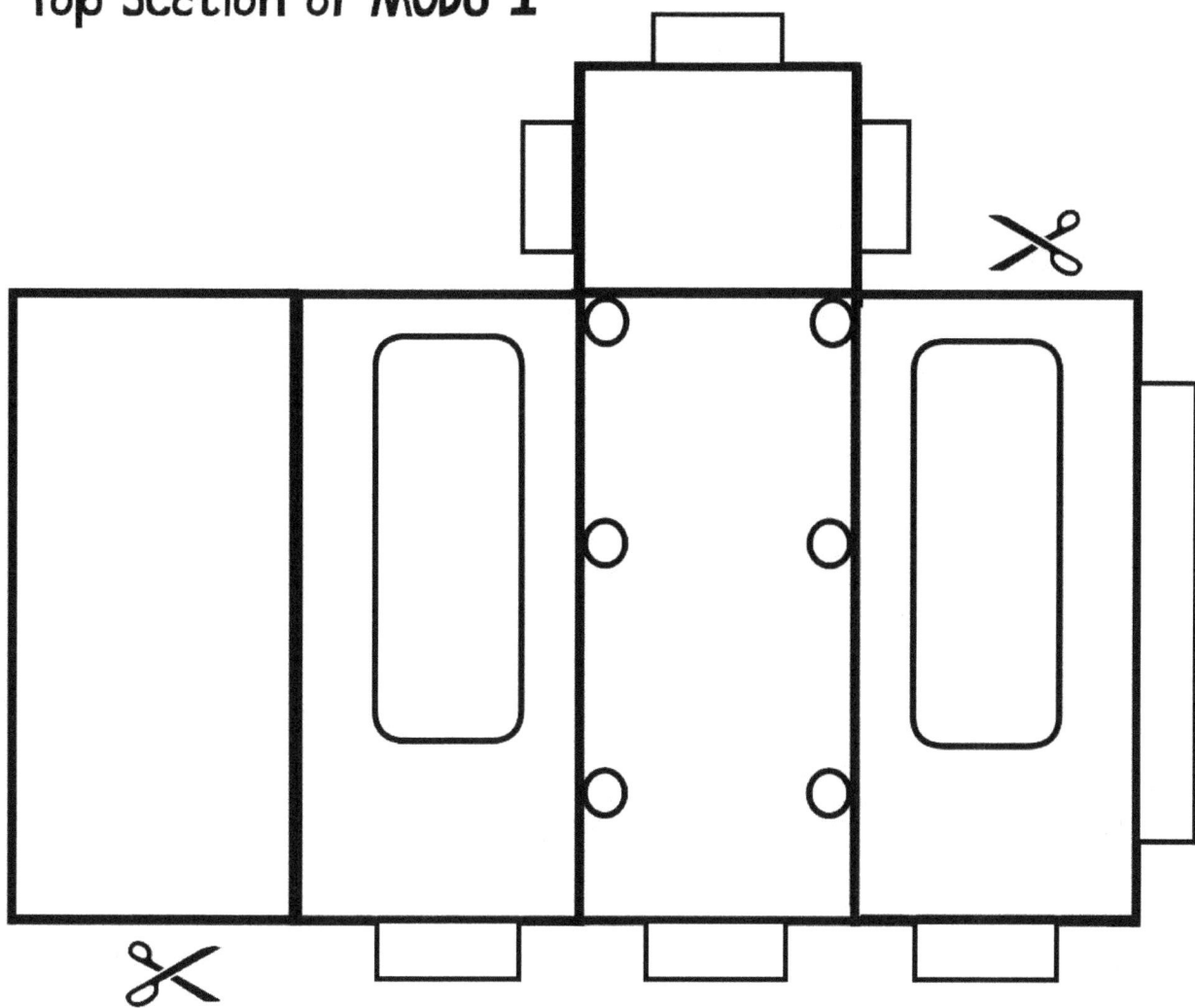

NOTE: Color before cutting!!!

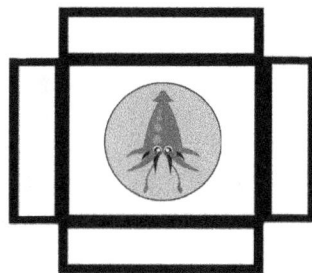

battery pack

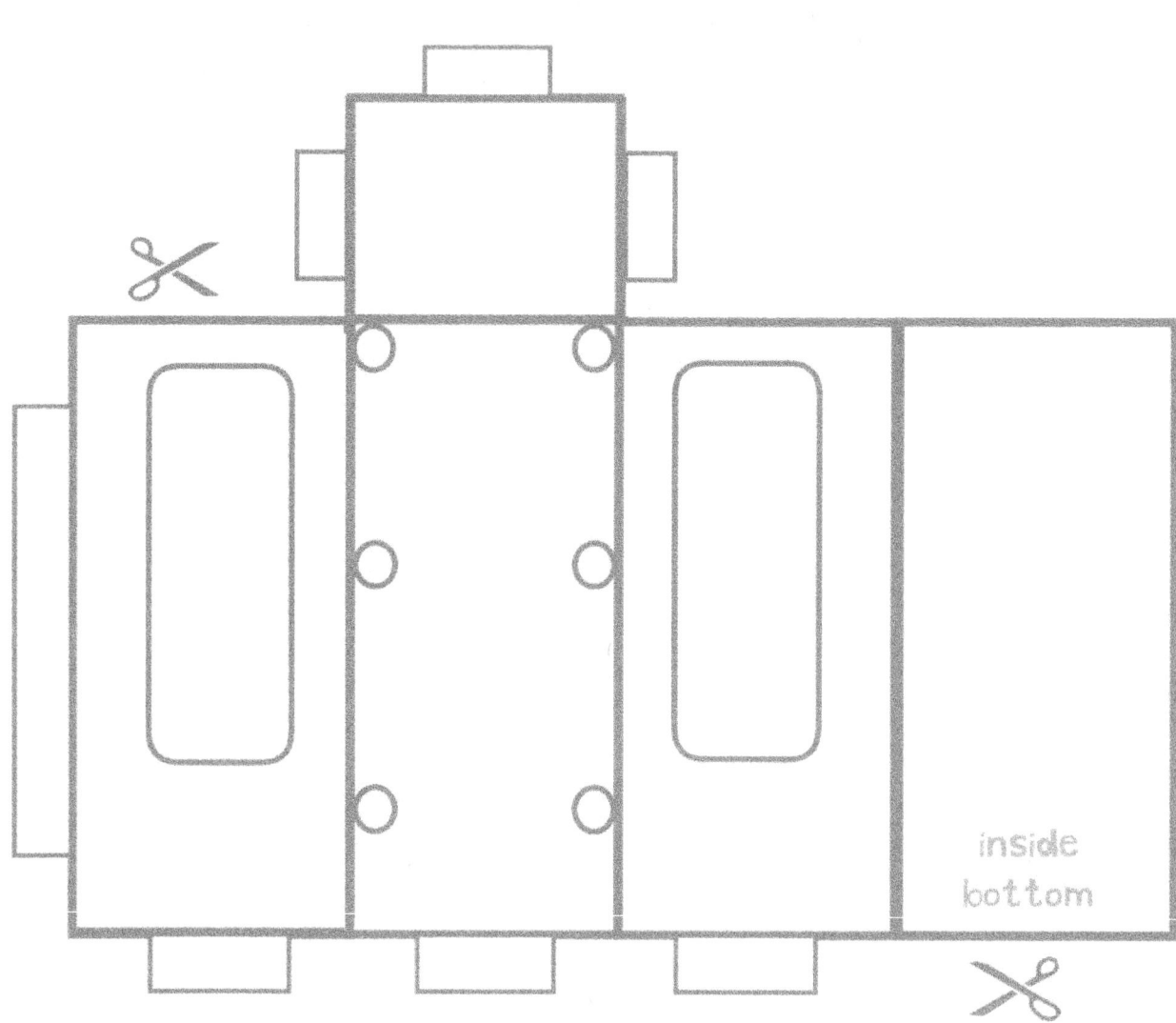

inside
bottom

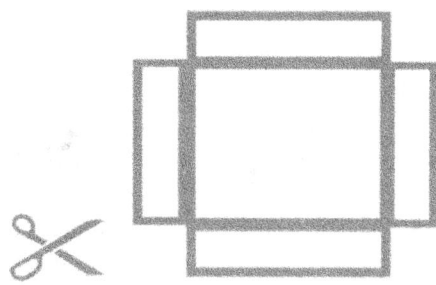

Bottom Section of MODU 1

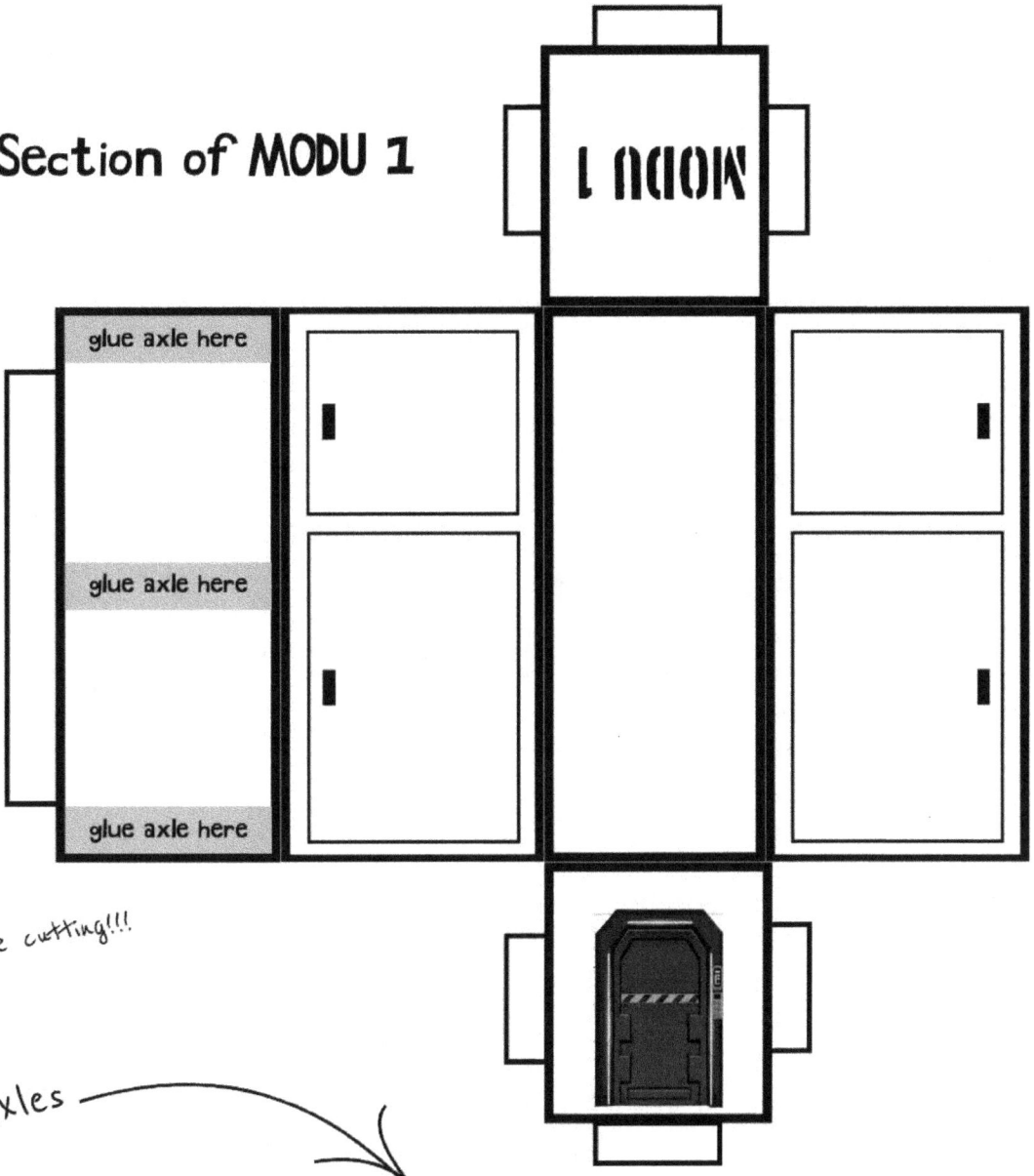

MODU 1

glue axle here

glue axle here

glue axle here

NOTE: Color before cutting!!!

The Axles

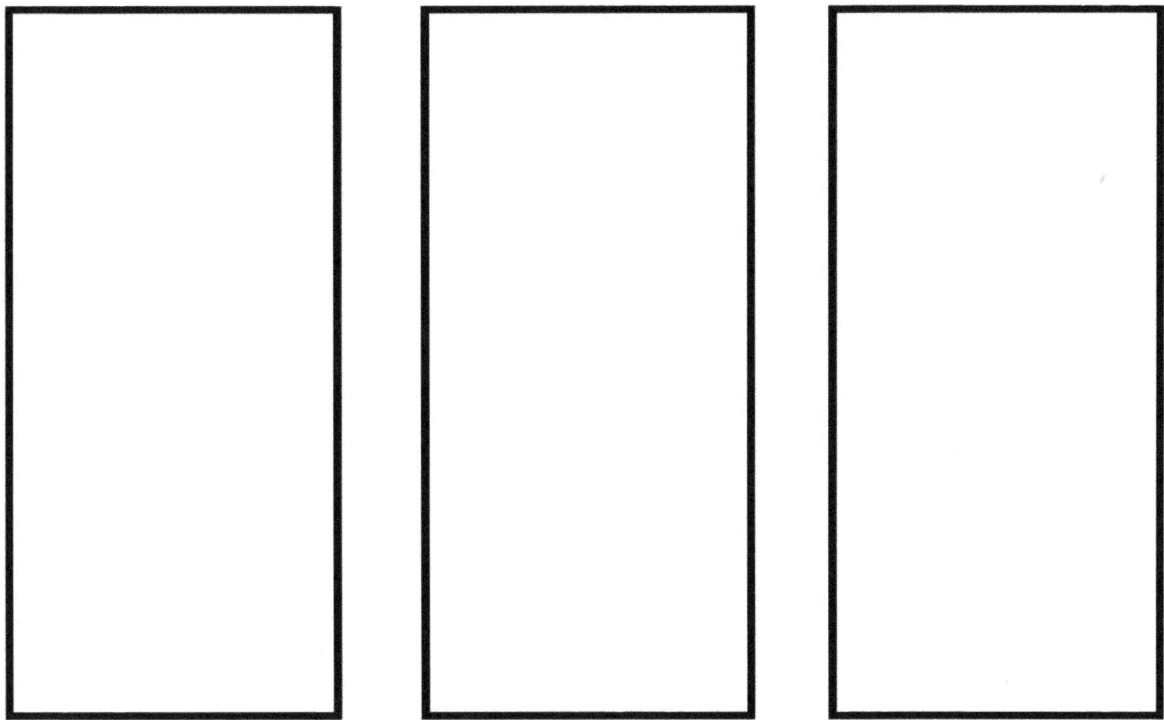

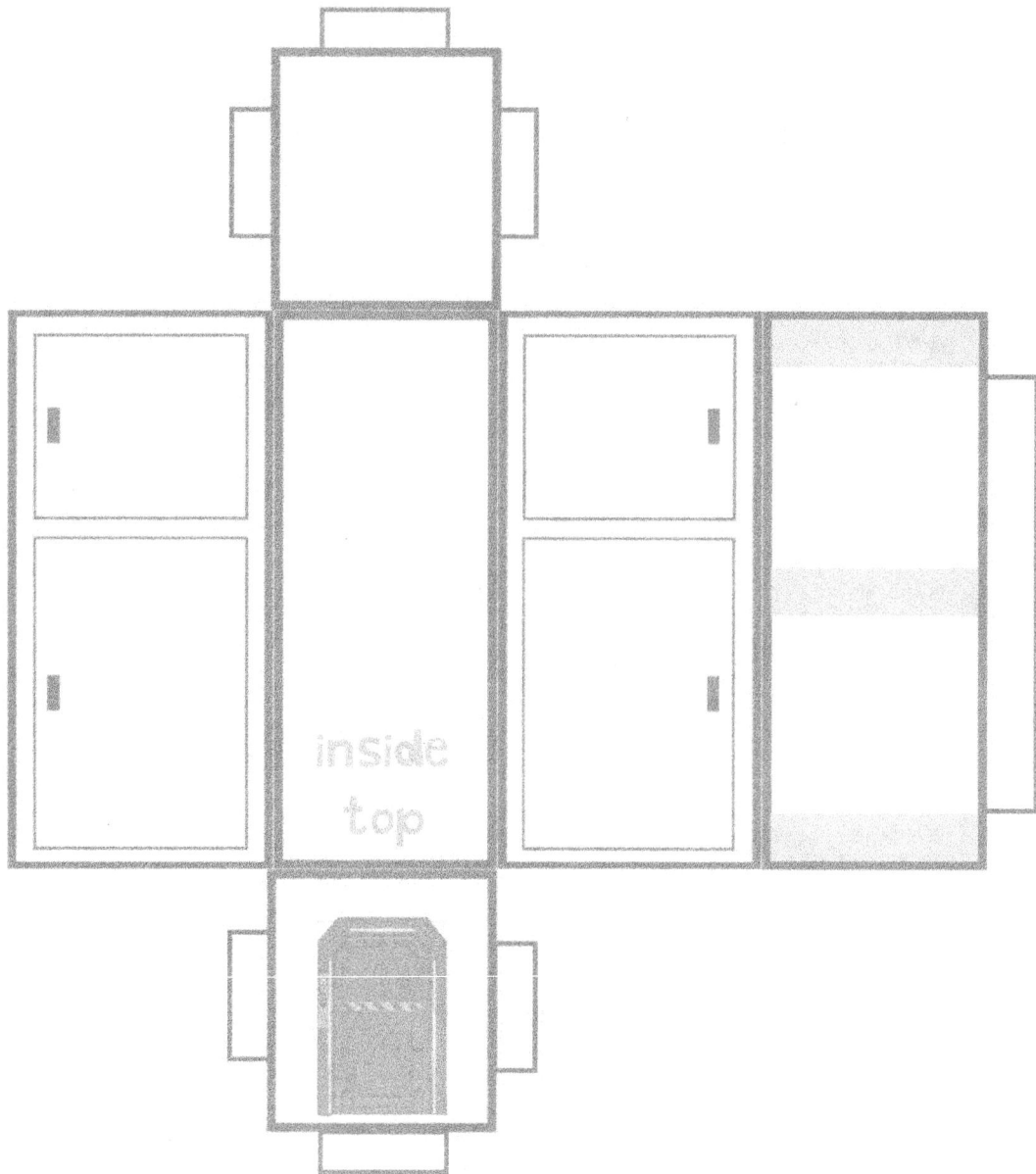

inside

top

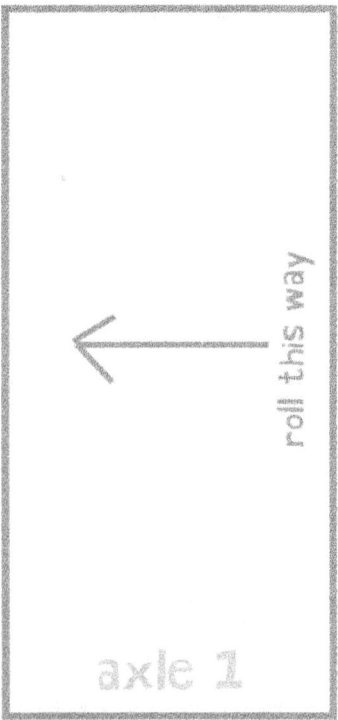

roll this way

axle 1

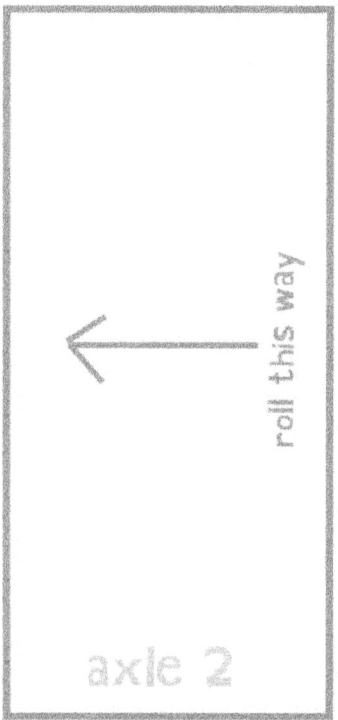

roll this way

axle 2

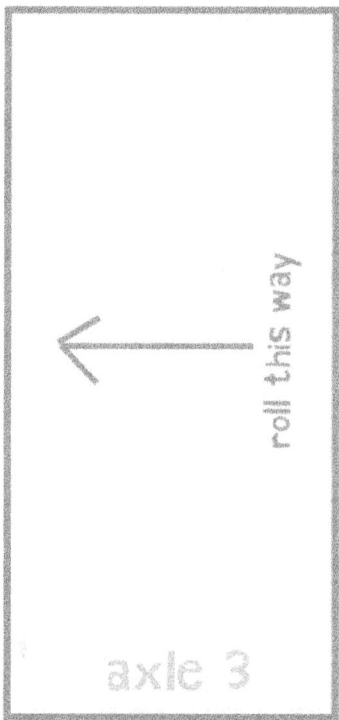

roll this way

axle 3

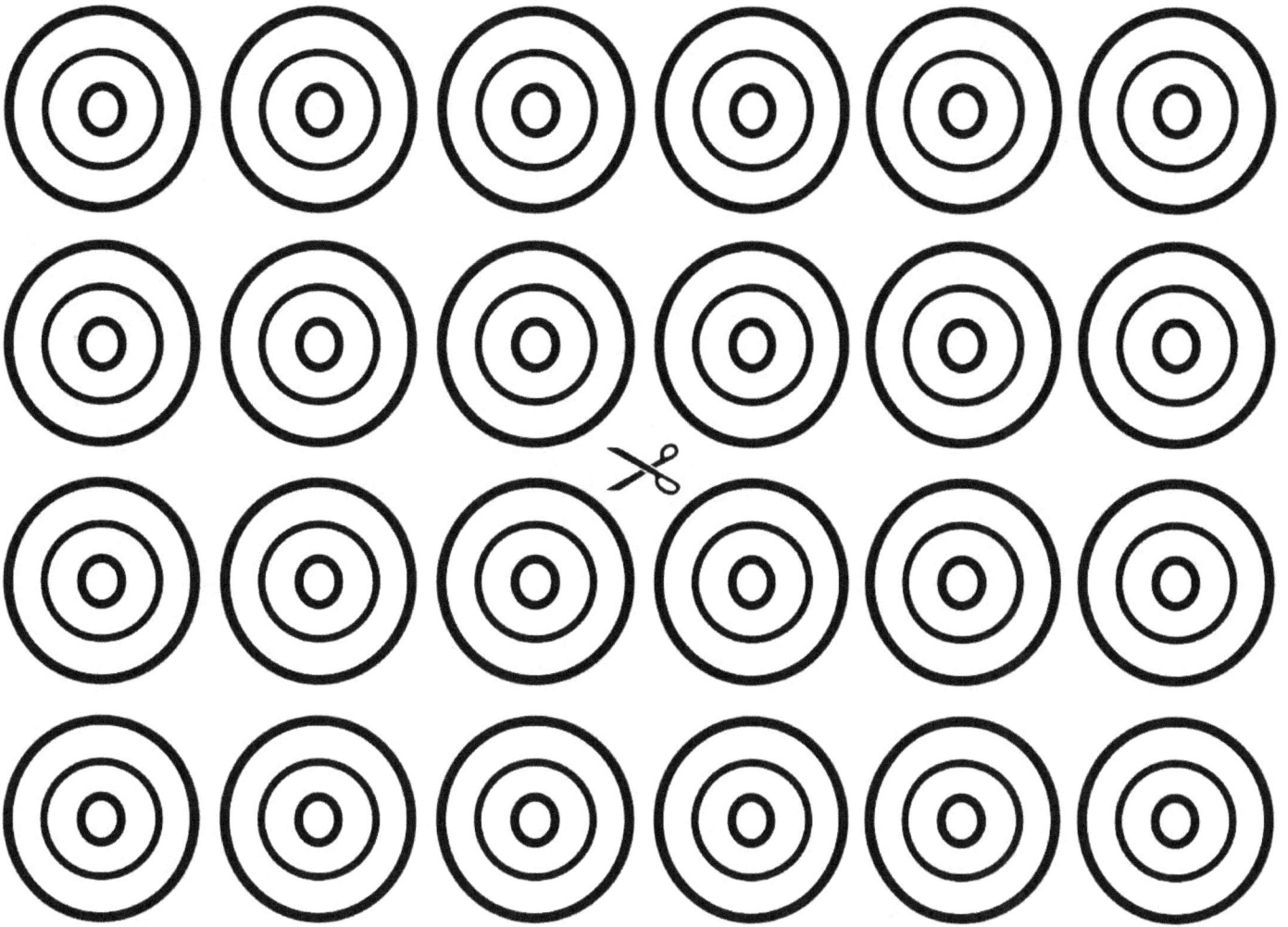

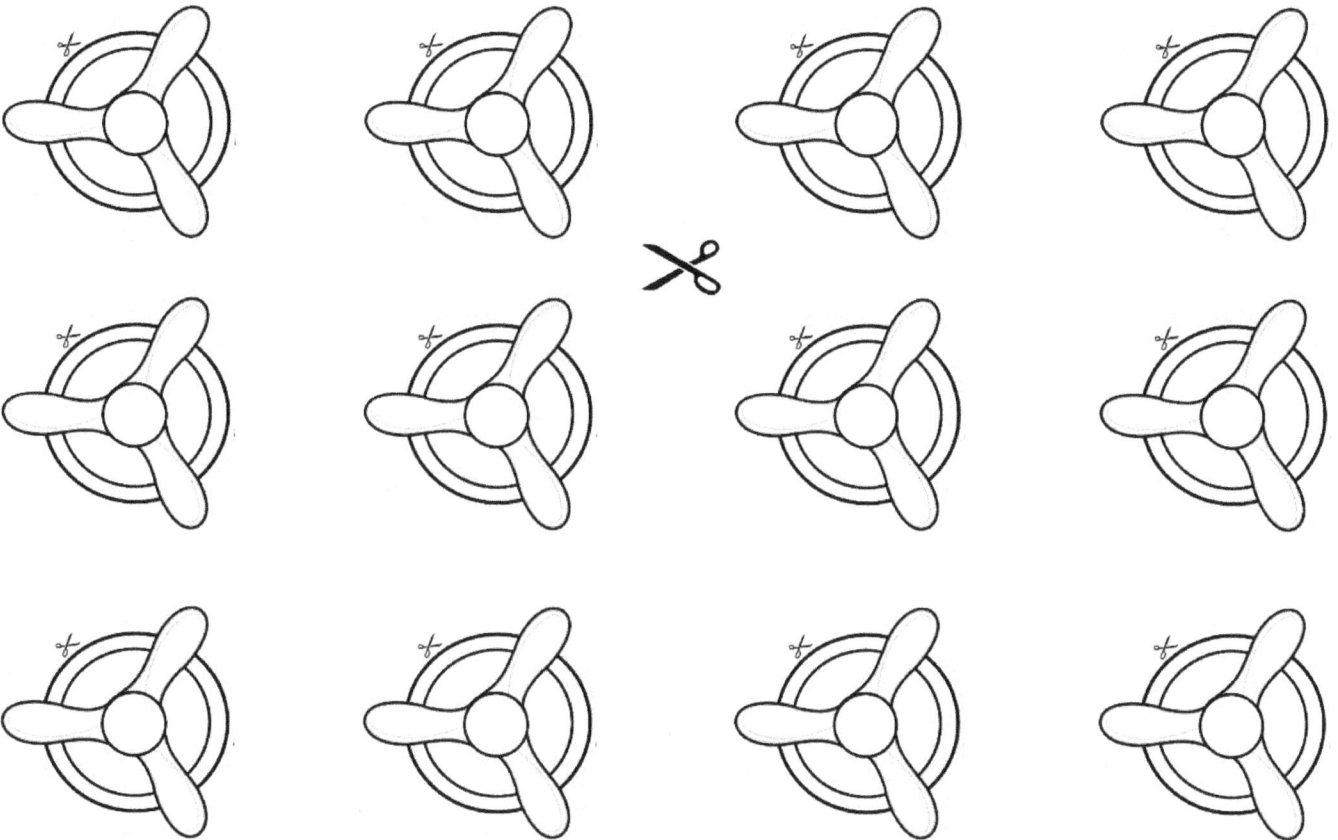

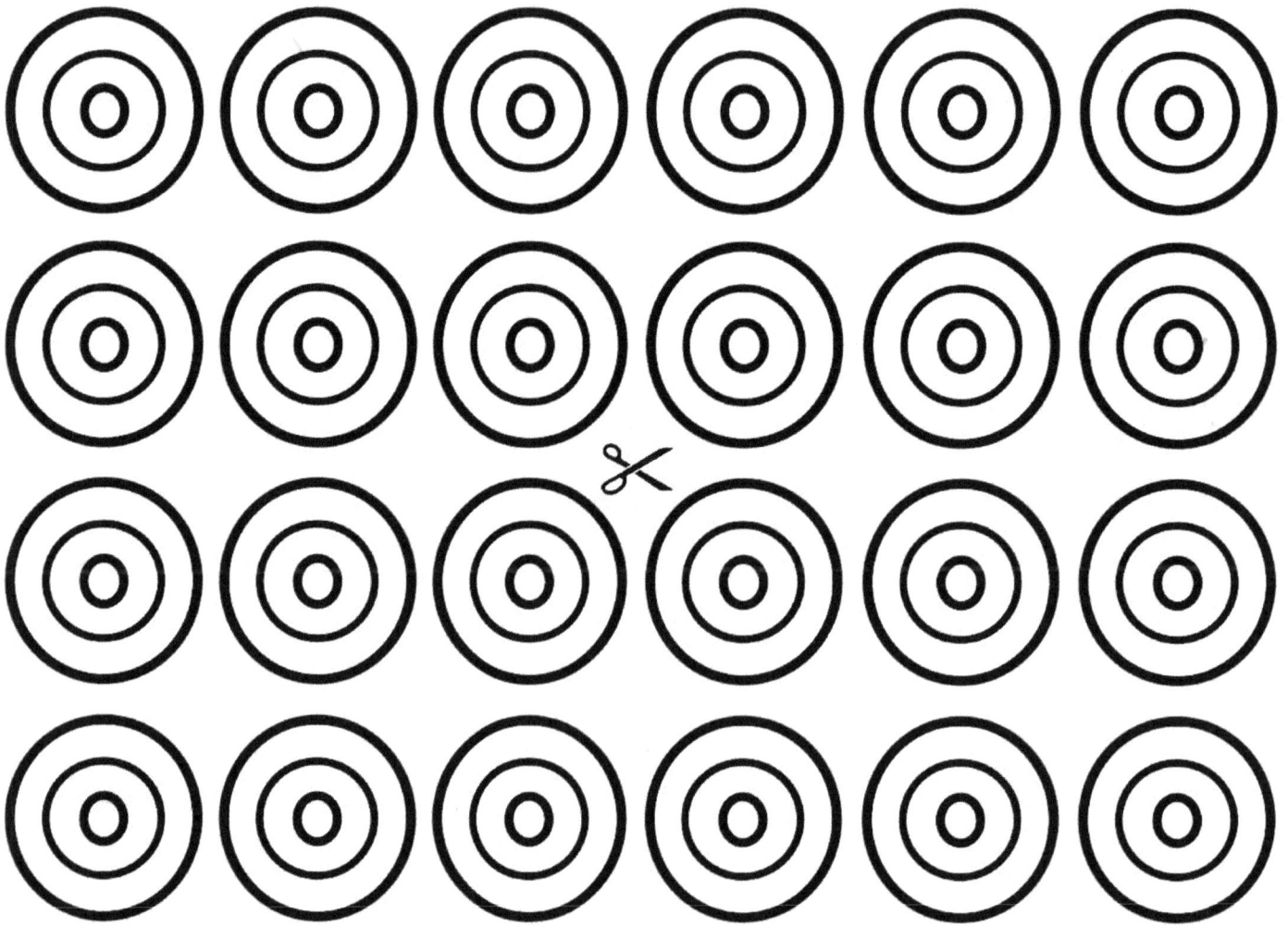

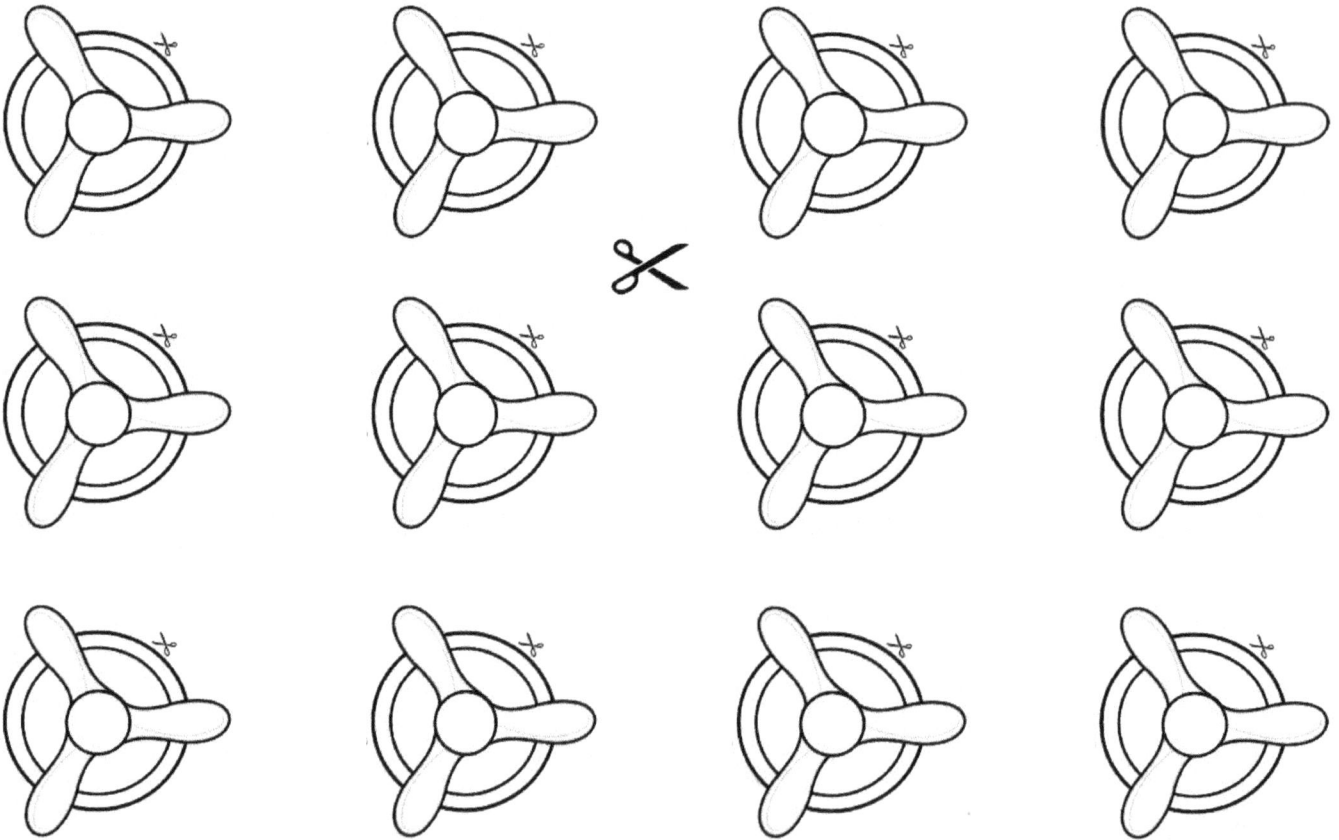

tire treads inside

tire treads inside

Top Section of MODU 3

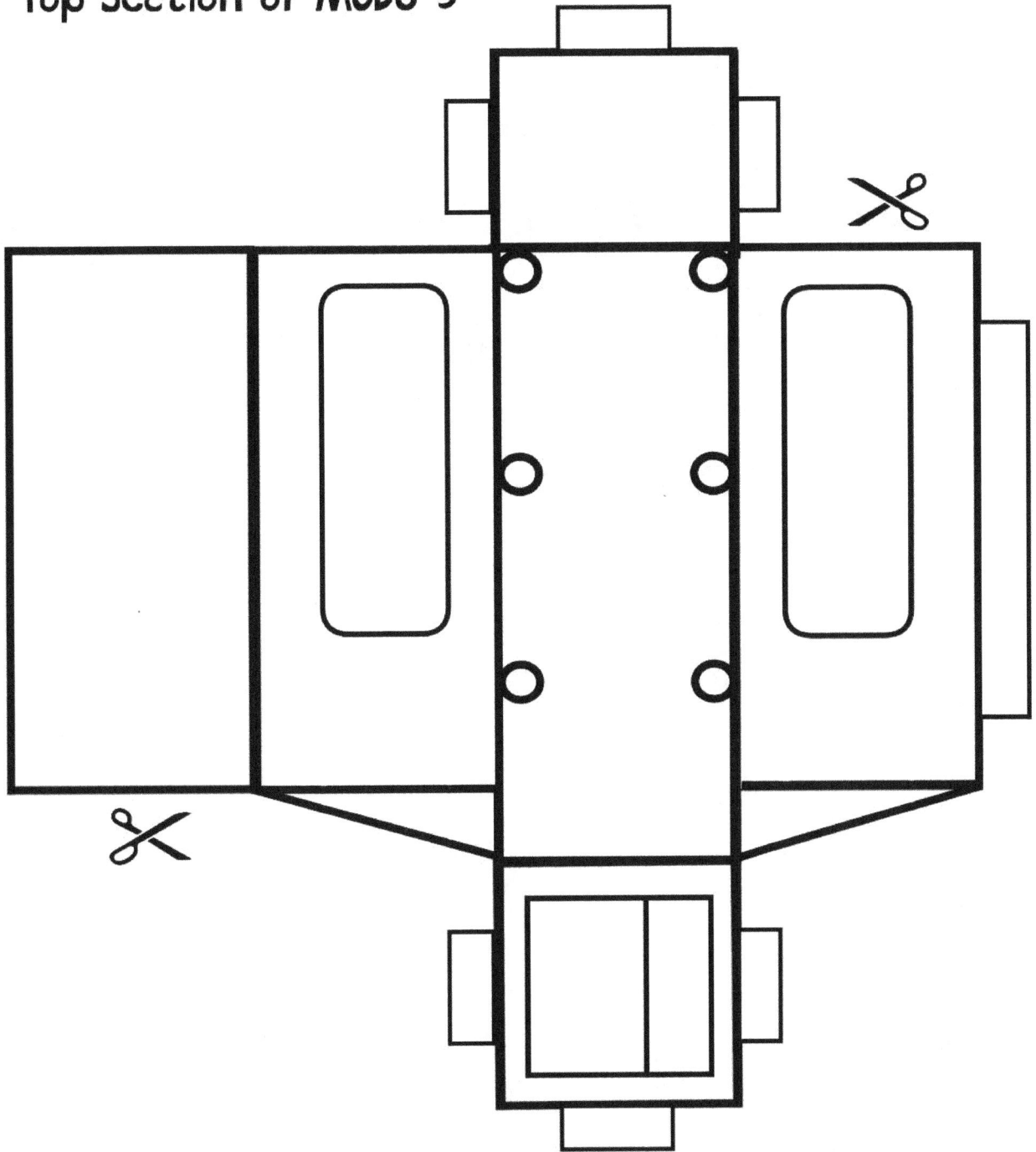

NOTE: Color before cutting!!!

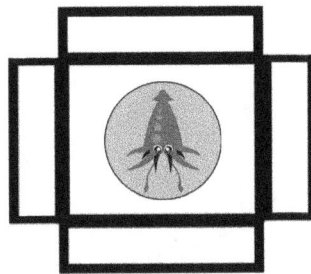

battery pack

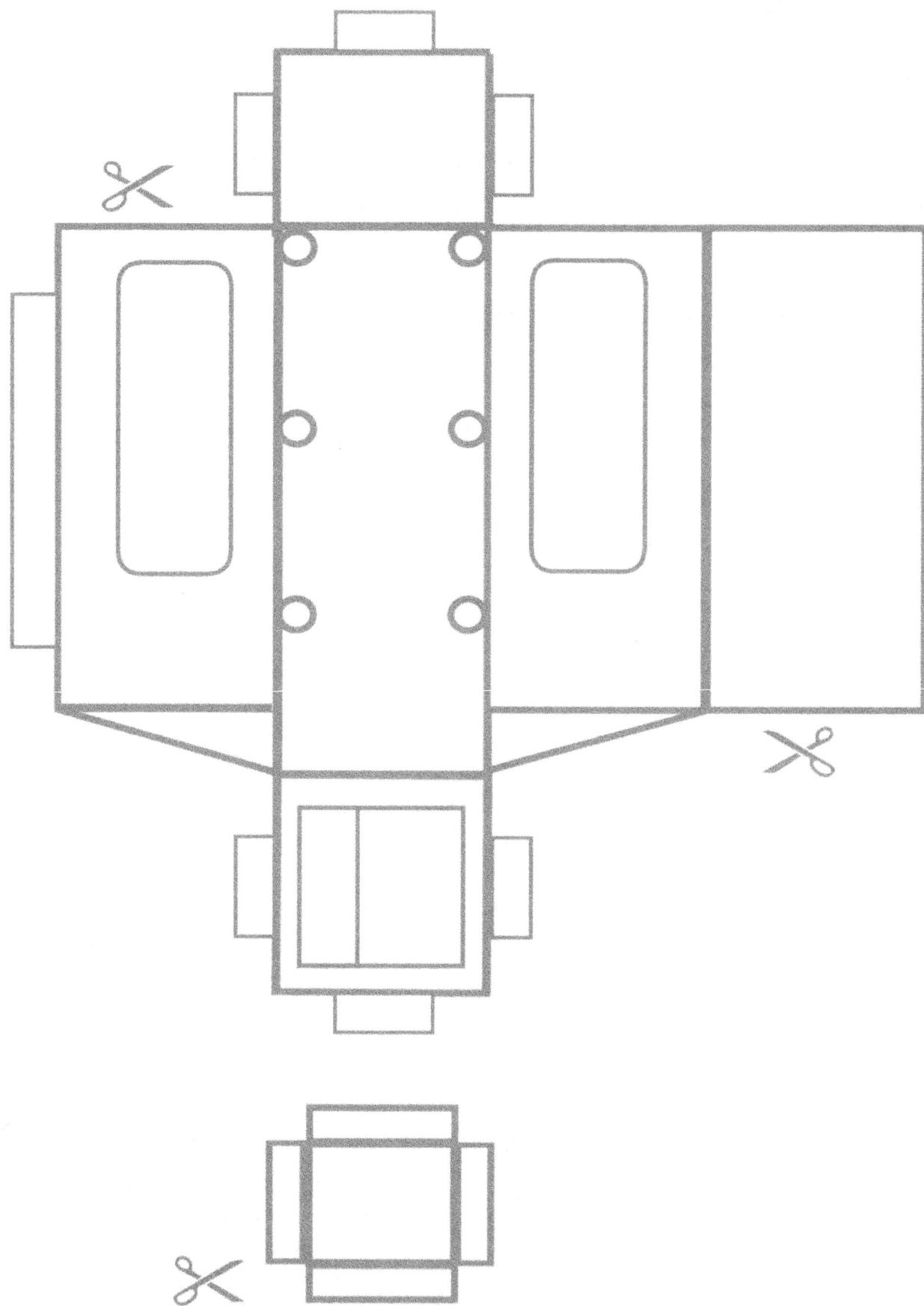

Bottom Section of MODU 3

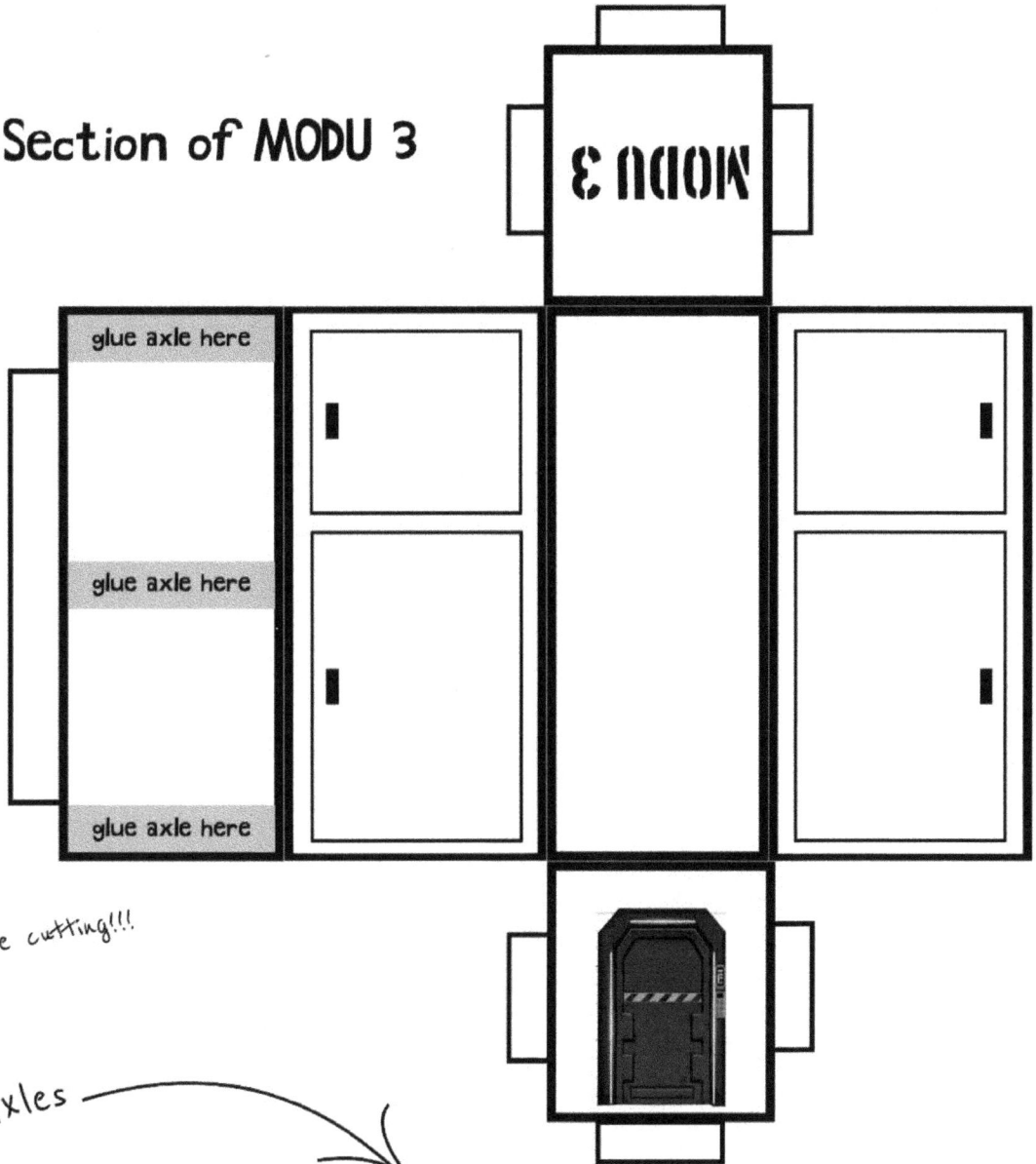

MODU 3

glue axle here

glue axle here

glue axle here

NOTE: Color before cutting!!!

The Axles

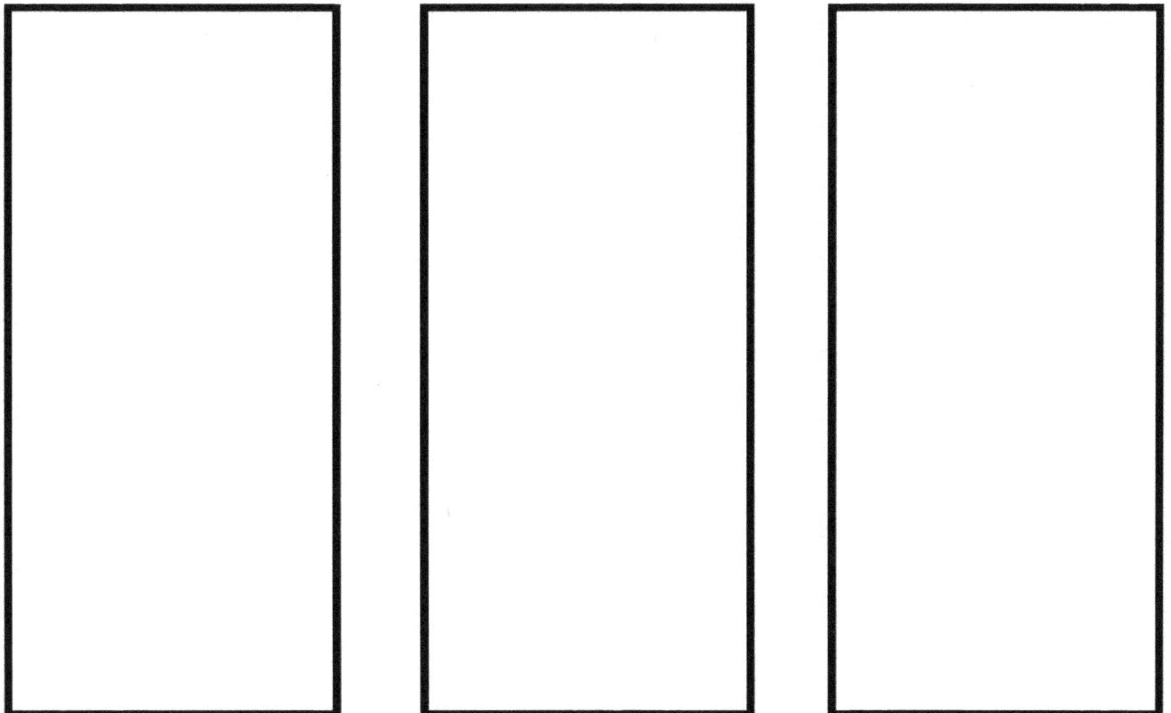

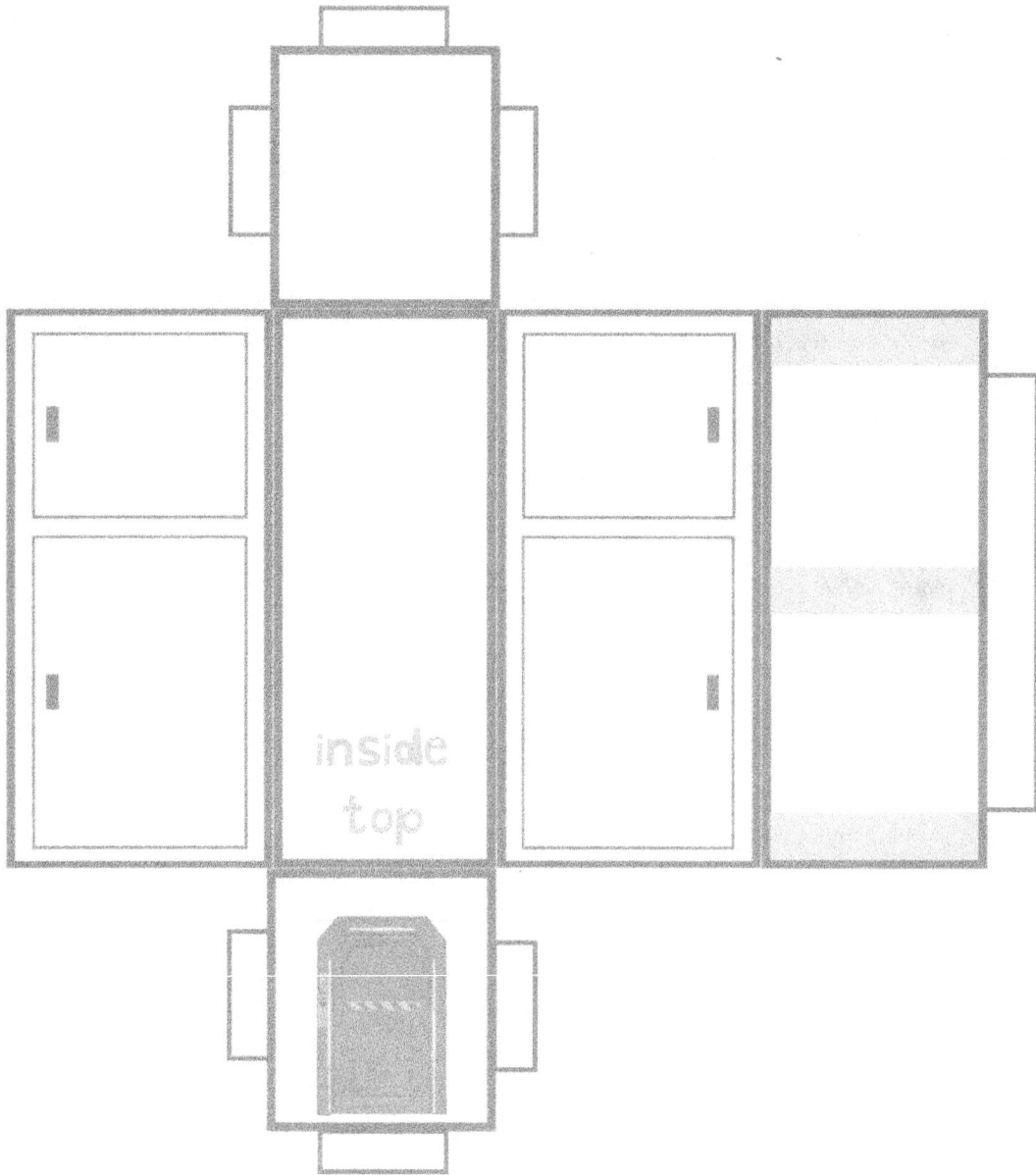

inside

top

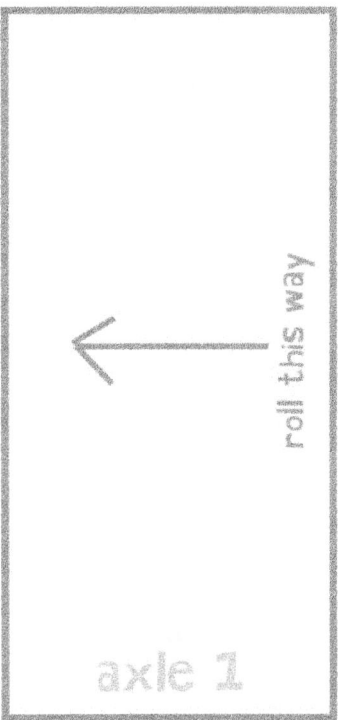

roll this way

axle 1

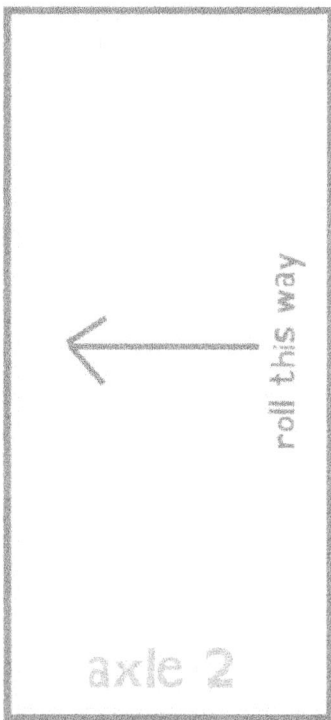

roll this way

axle 2

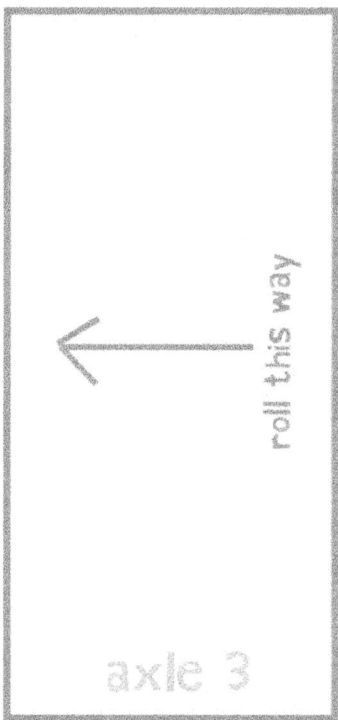

roll this way

axle 3

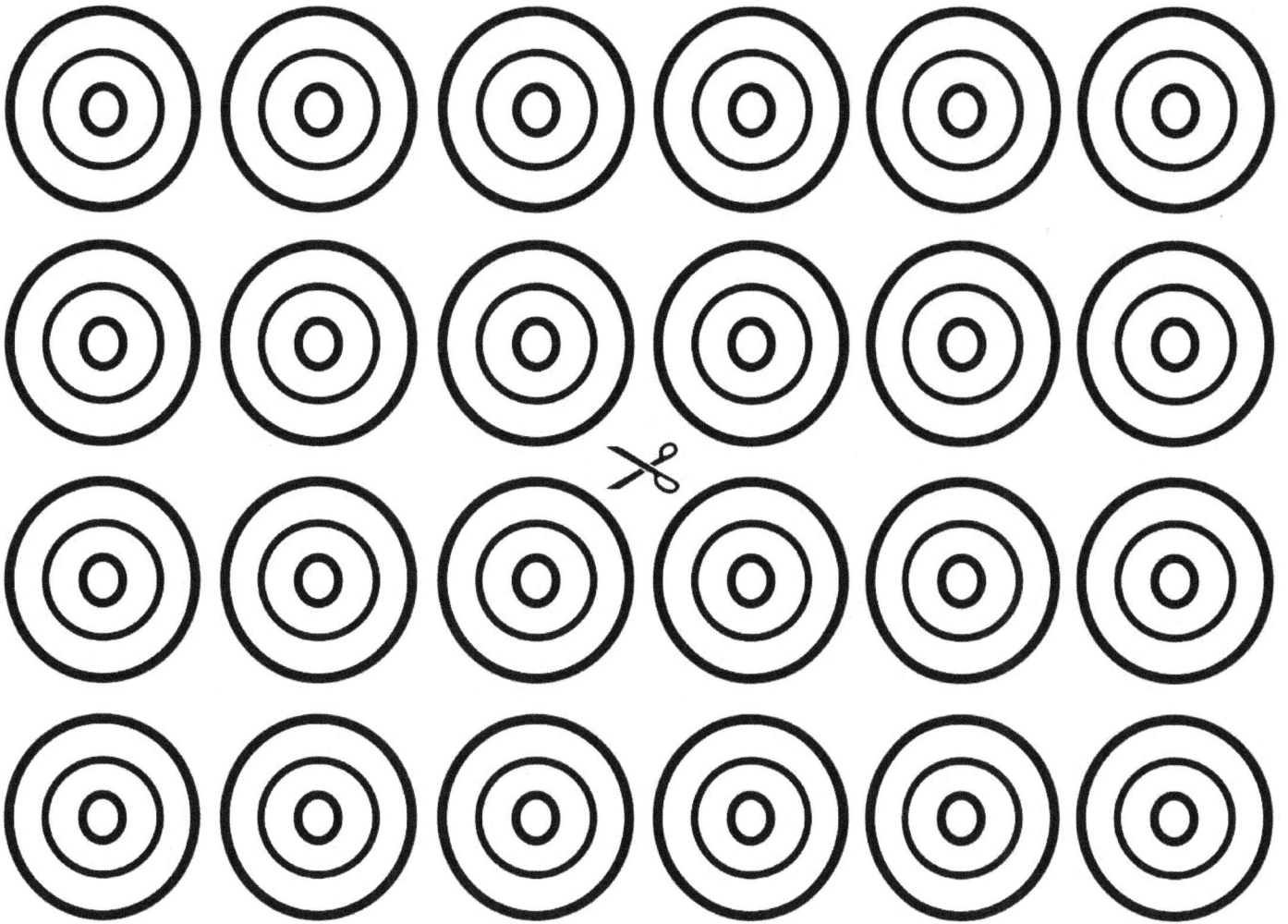

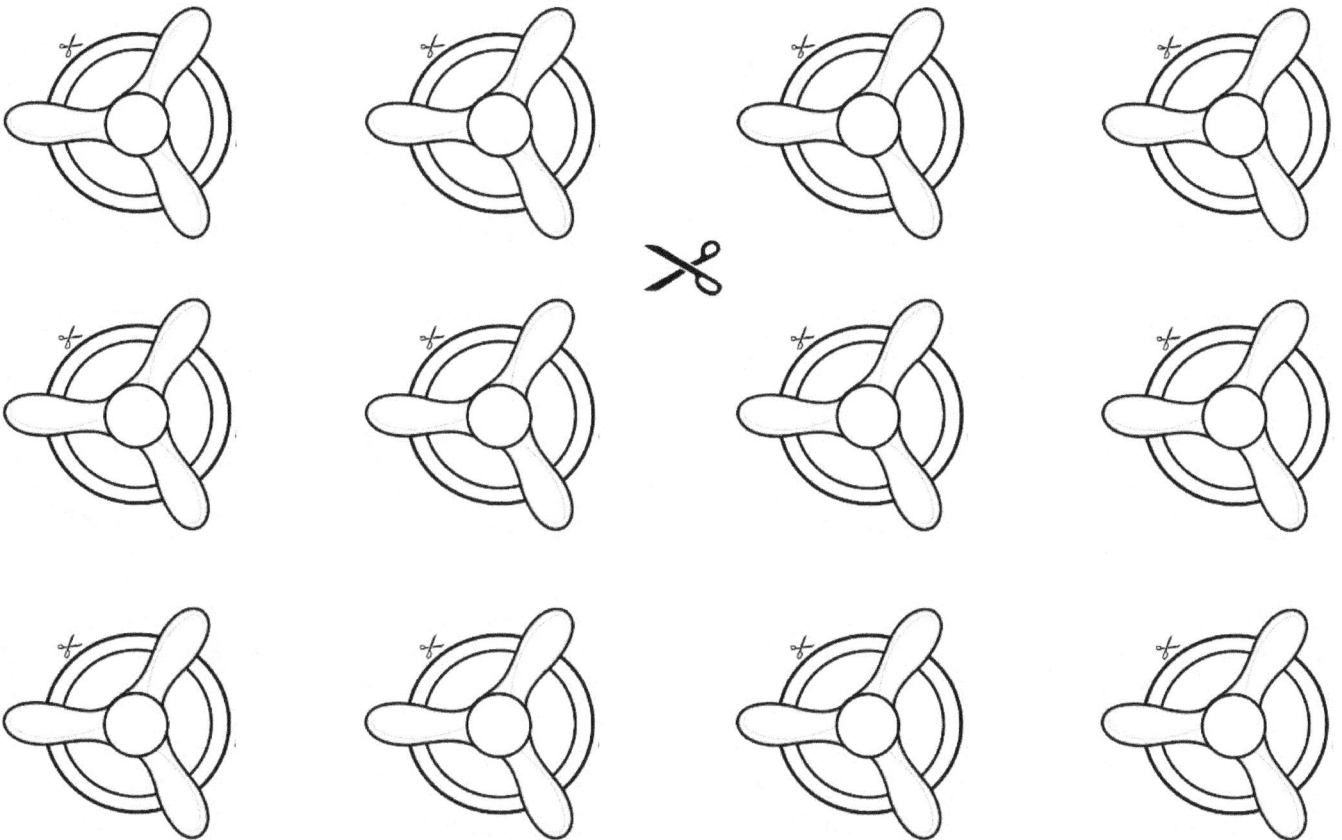

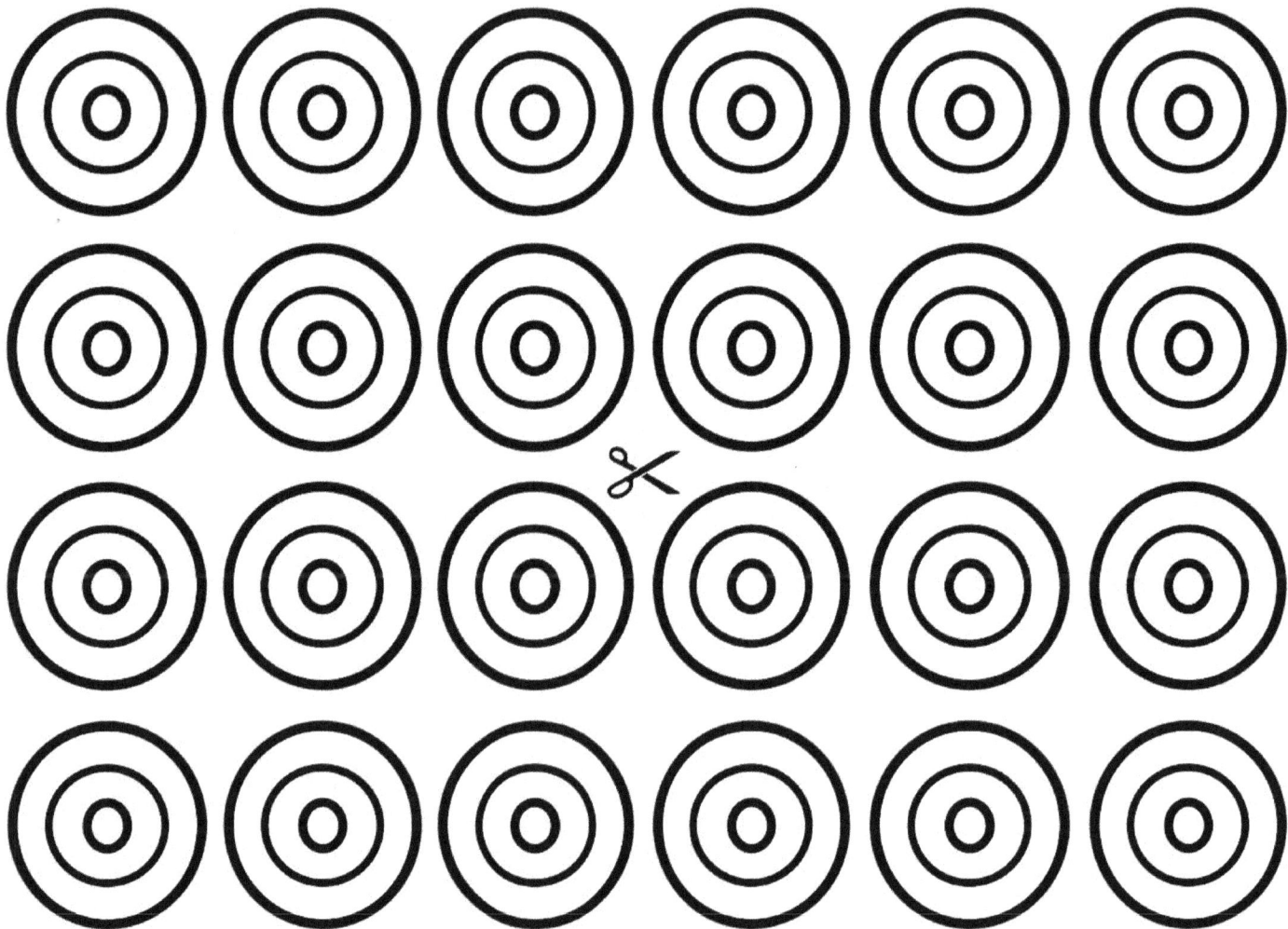

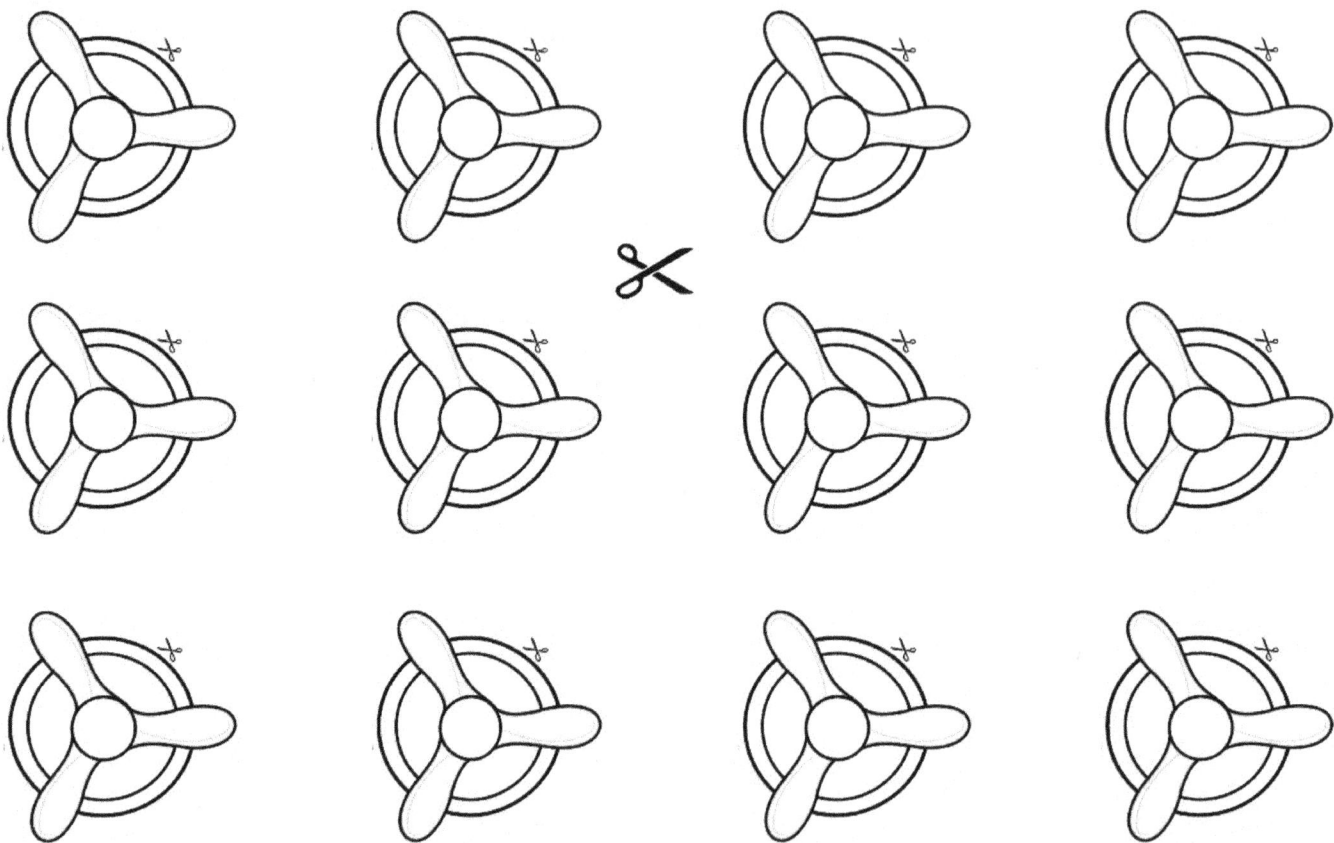

tire treads inside

tire treads inside

THE
MODEL
SHOP

(for all you extra model part needs)

Models can be made from almost anything like wood, metal, and foam board (heck, I once made a model out of a bar of soap). But in our case we are using paper and you know that paper can rip easily. That's why this model shop exists, in case of mistakes. If no mistakes were made architect, you could try building another model with the pieces if you like. Maybe change the shape a bit or the color. It's entirely up to you!

MODU 1

MODU 2

MODU 3

GLUE THIS SIDE TO THE BASE

(bottom)

Front and Roof of The Port

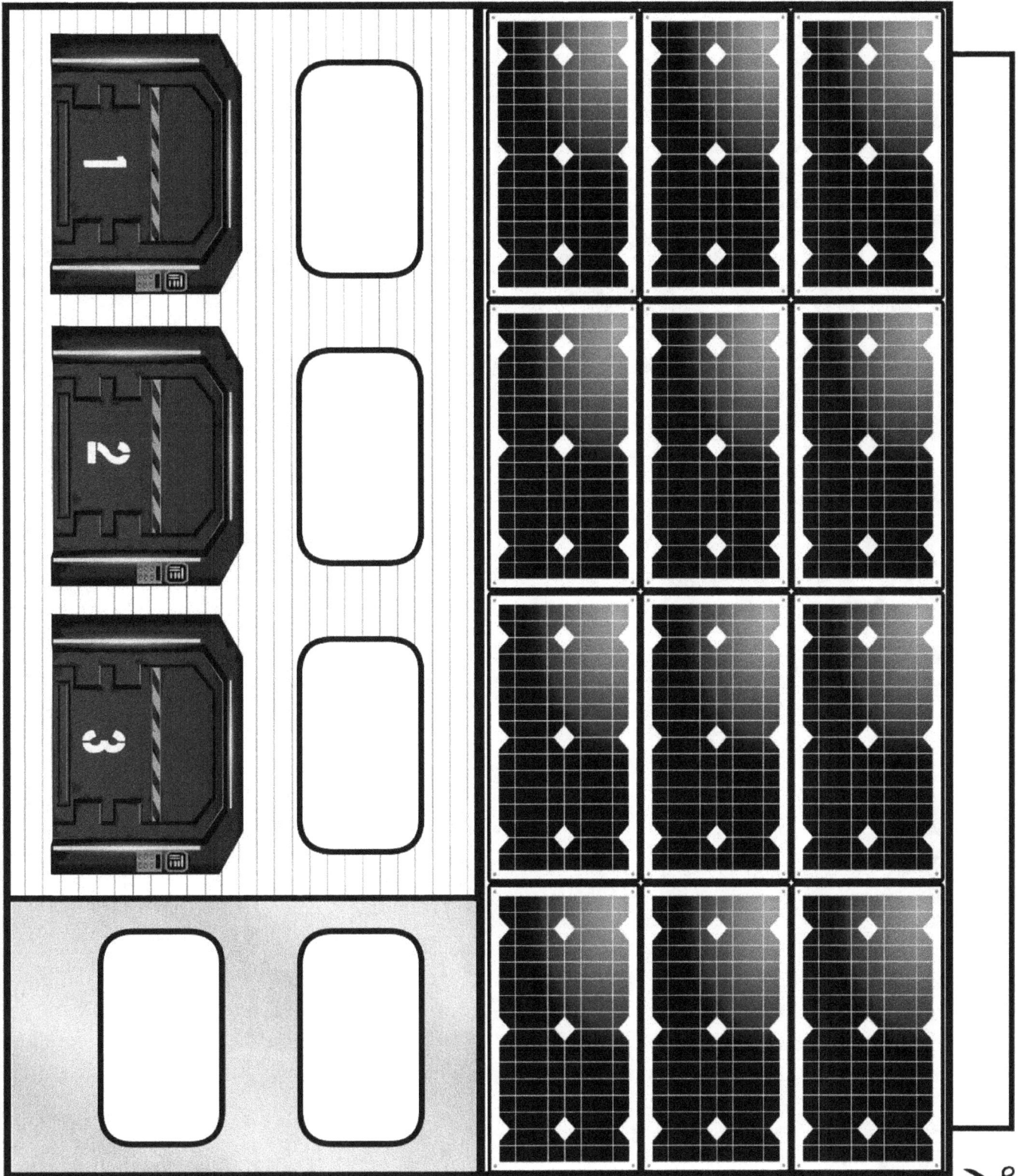

NOTE: The walls/roof are made with layers of red regolith so if you wanna color them, now is a good time!!!

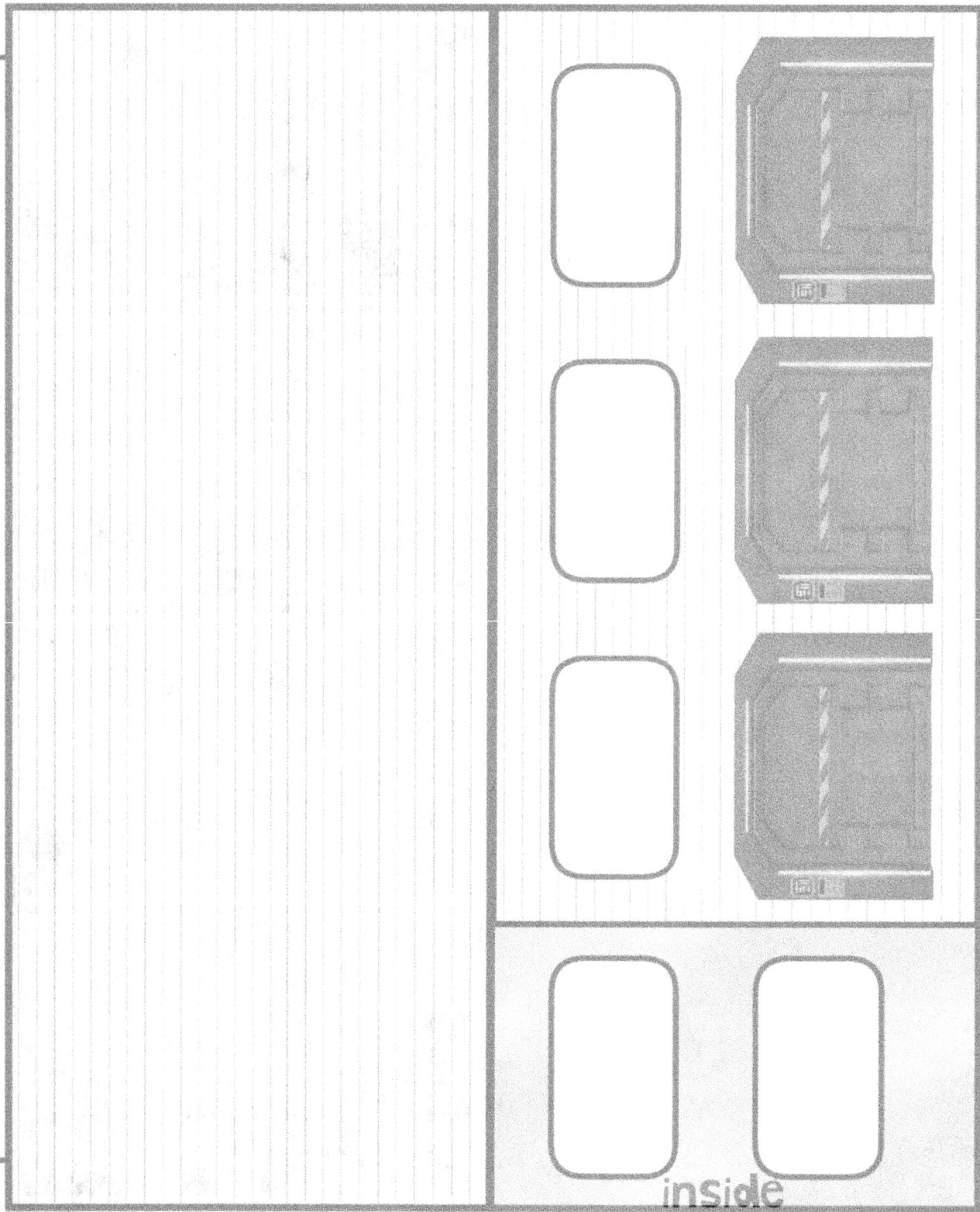

inside

Back and Underside of The Port

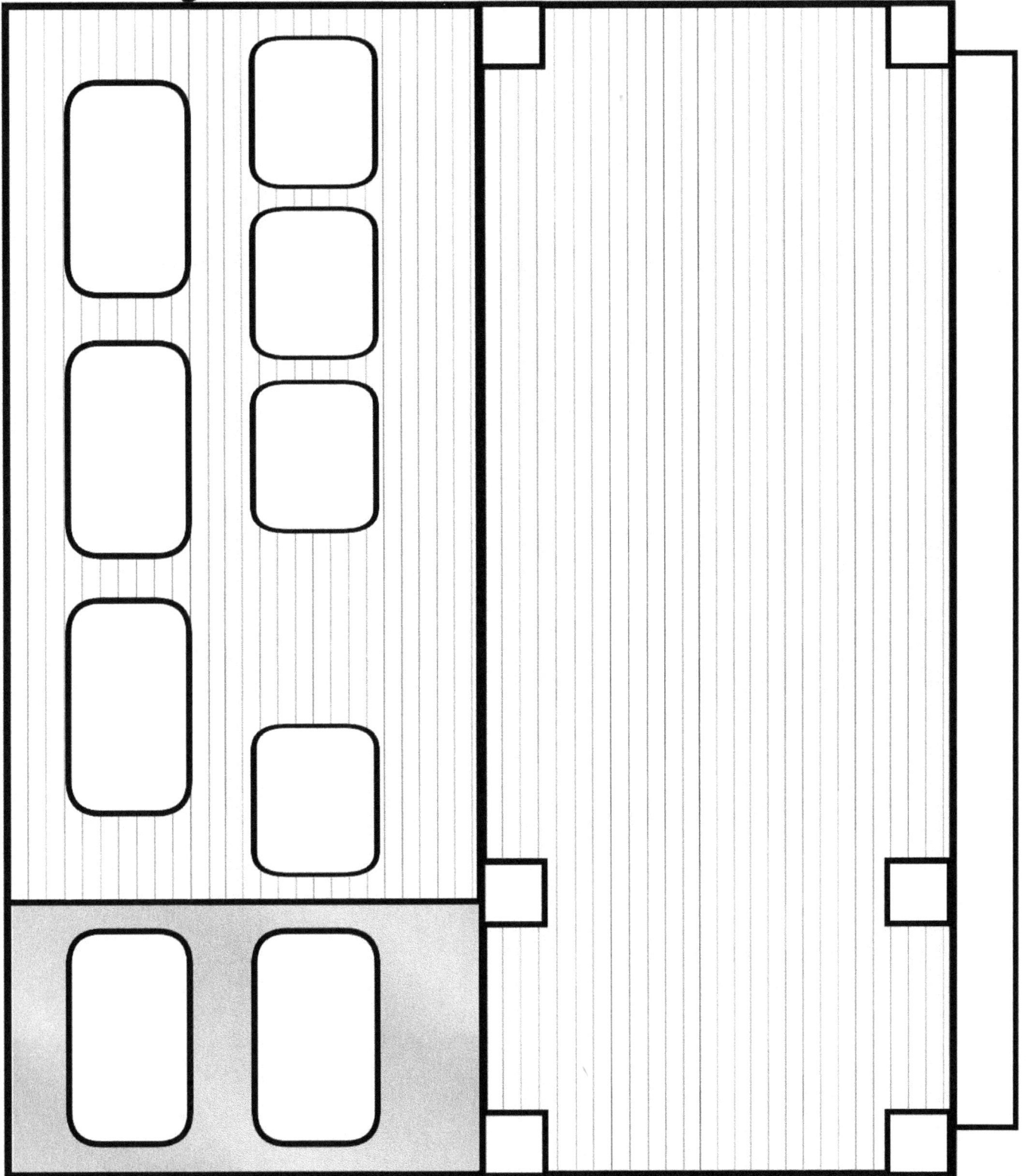

NOTE: The walls/underside are made with layers of red regolith so if you wanna color them, now is a good time!!!

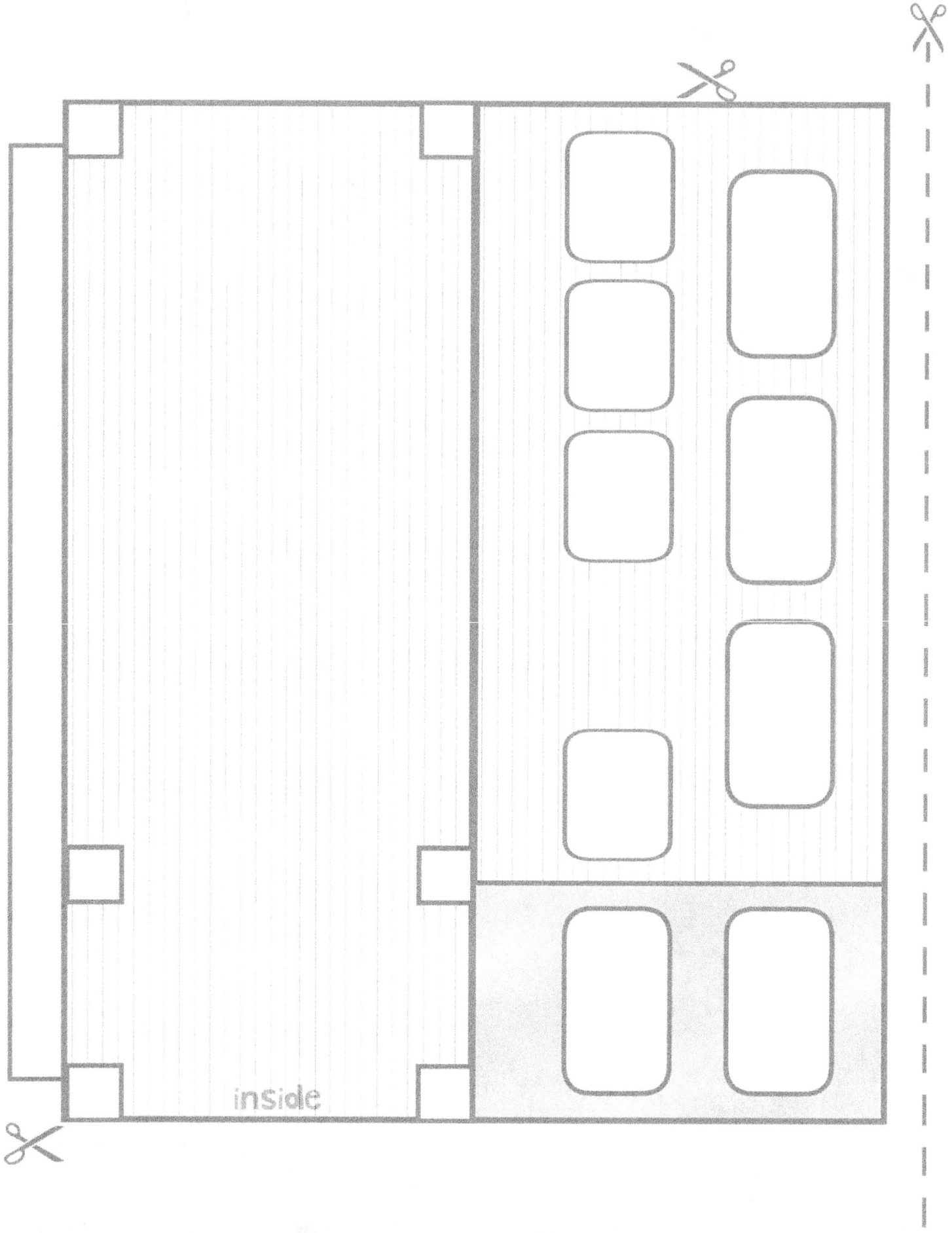

inside

NOTE: Color before cutting!!!

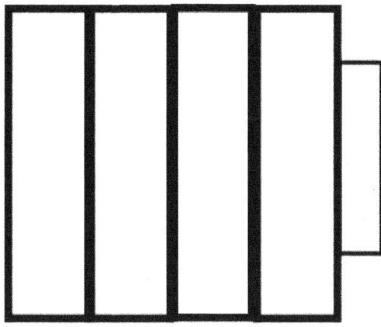

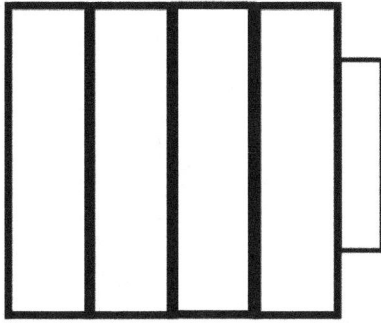

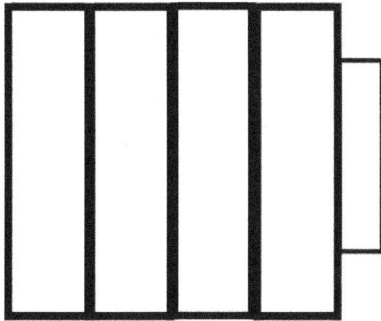

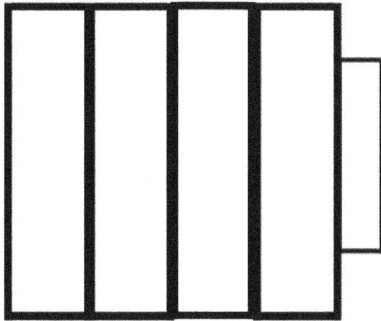

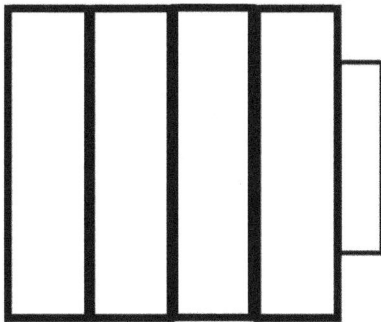

columns

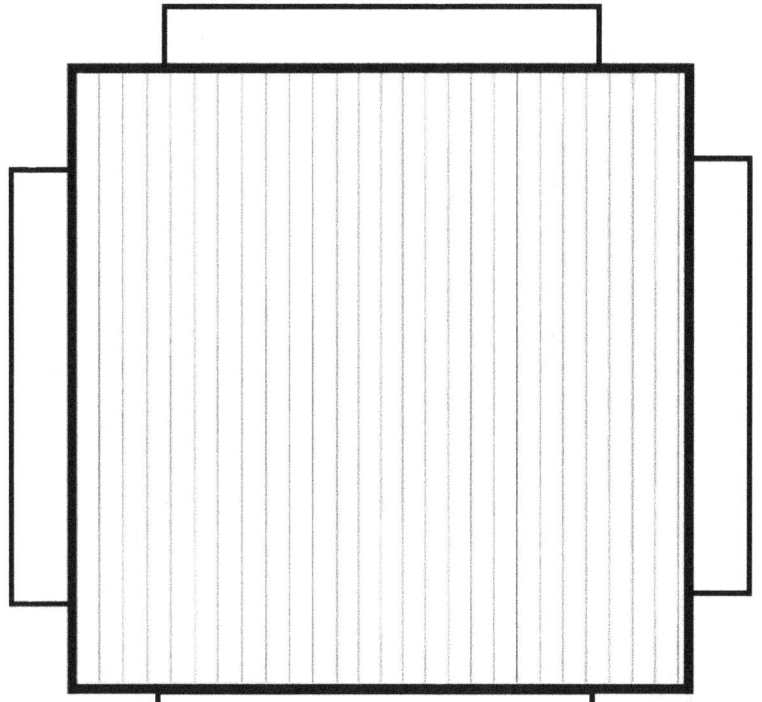

Port
Side
Walls

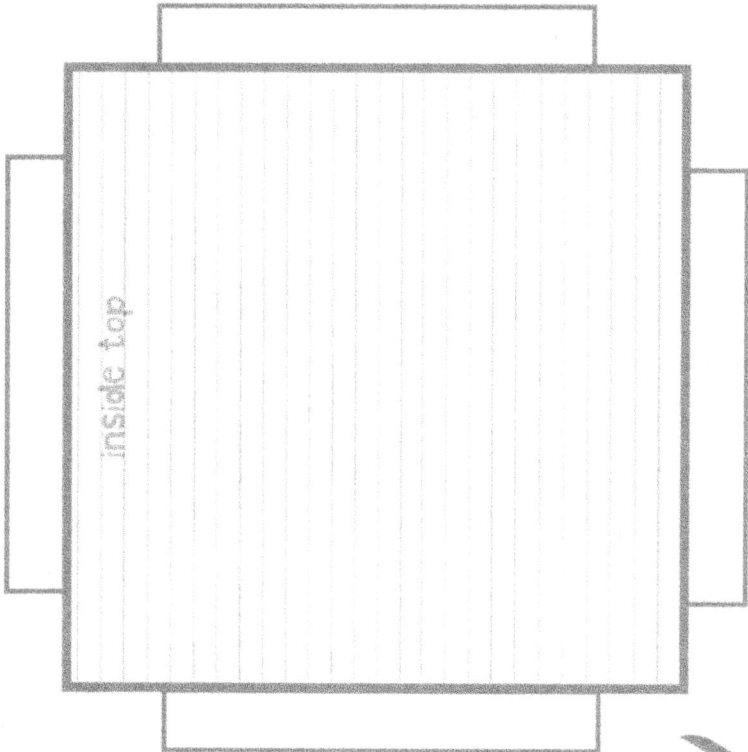

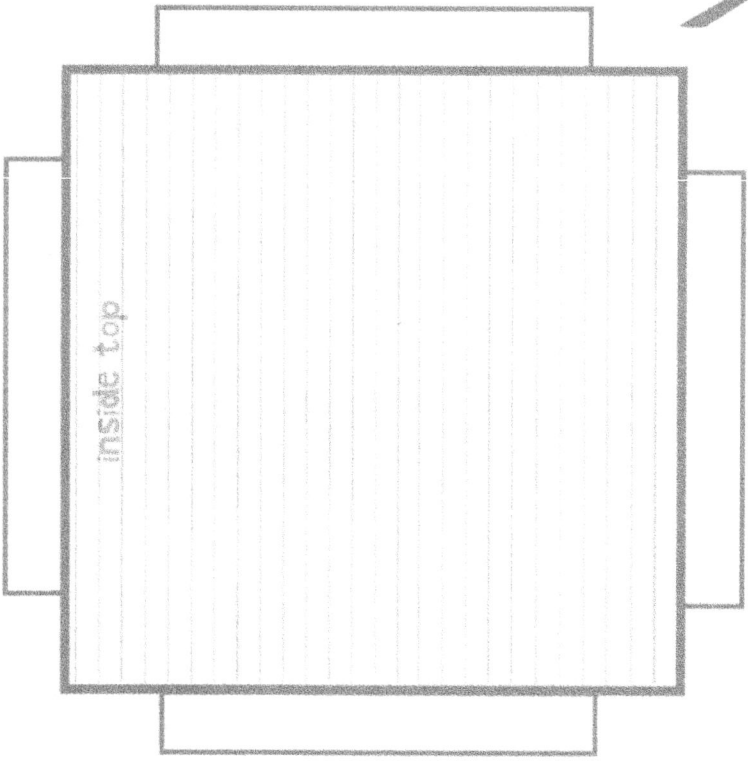

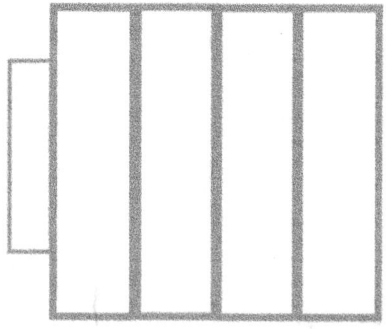

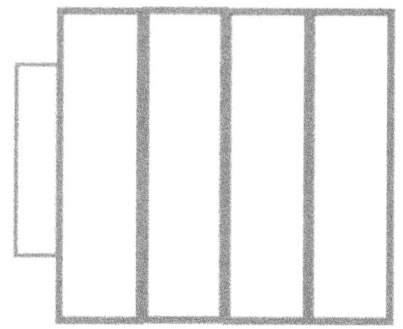

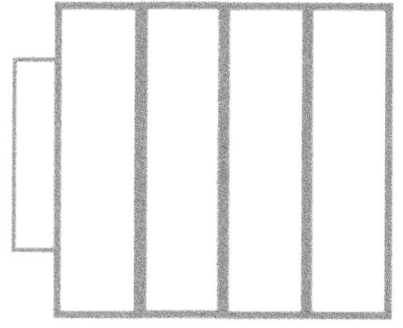

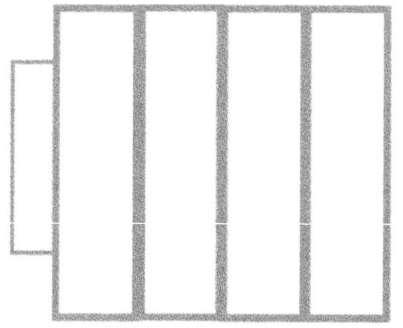

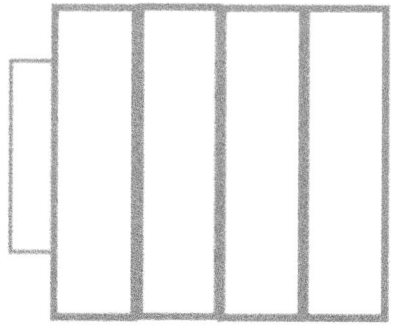

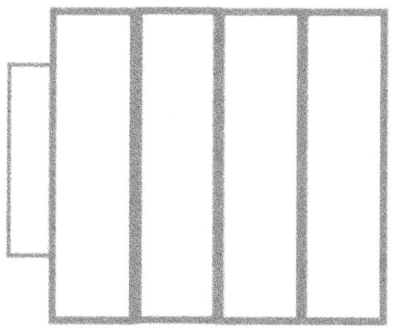

inside top

inside top

Top Section of MODU 1

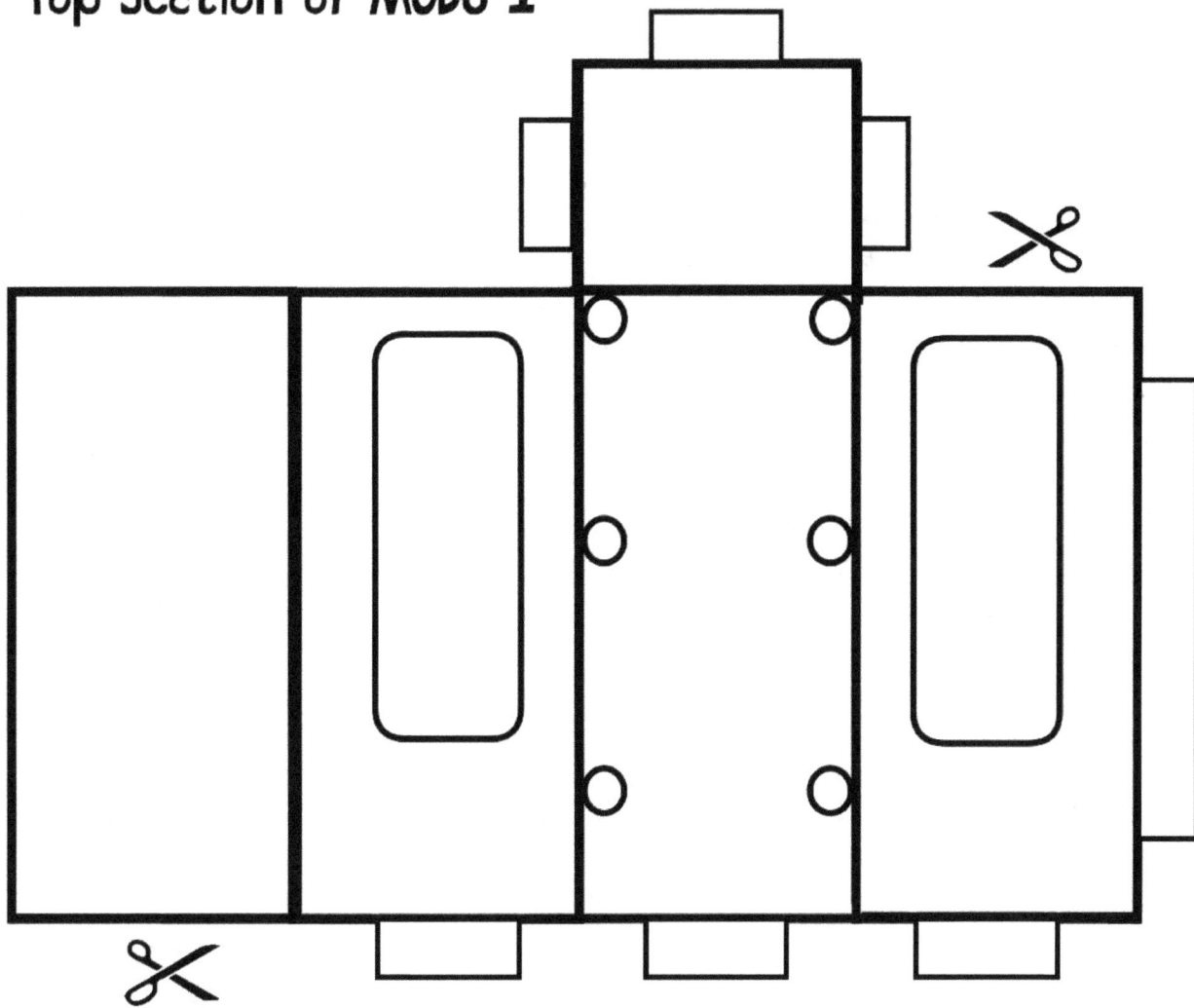

NOTE: Color before cutting!!!

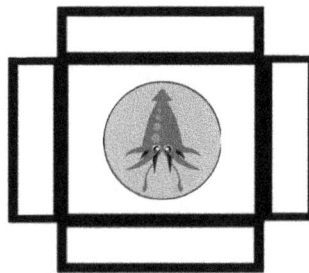

battery pack

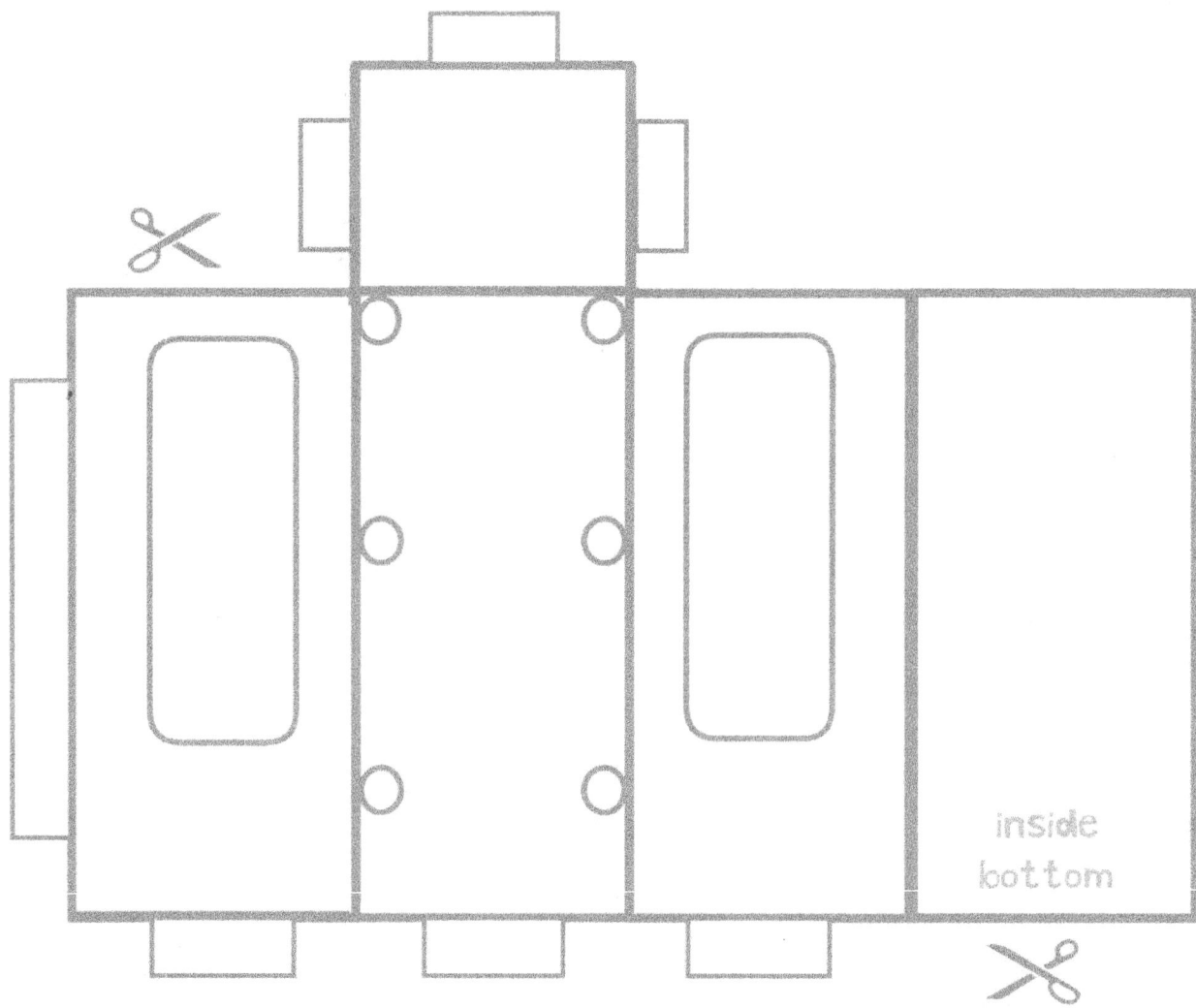

inside
bottom

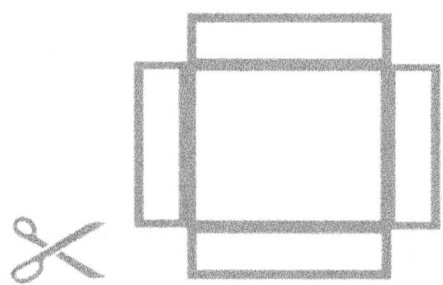

Bottom Section of MODU 1

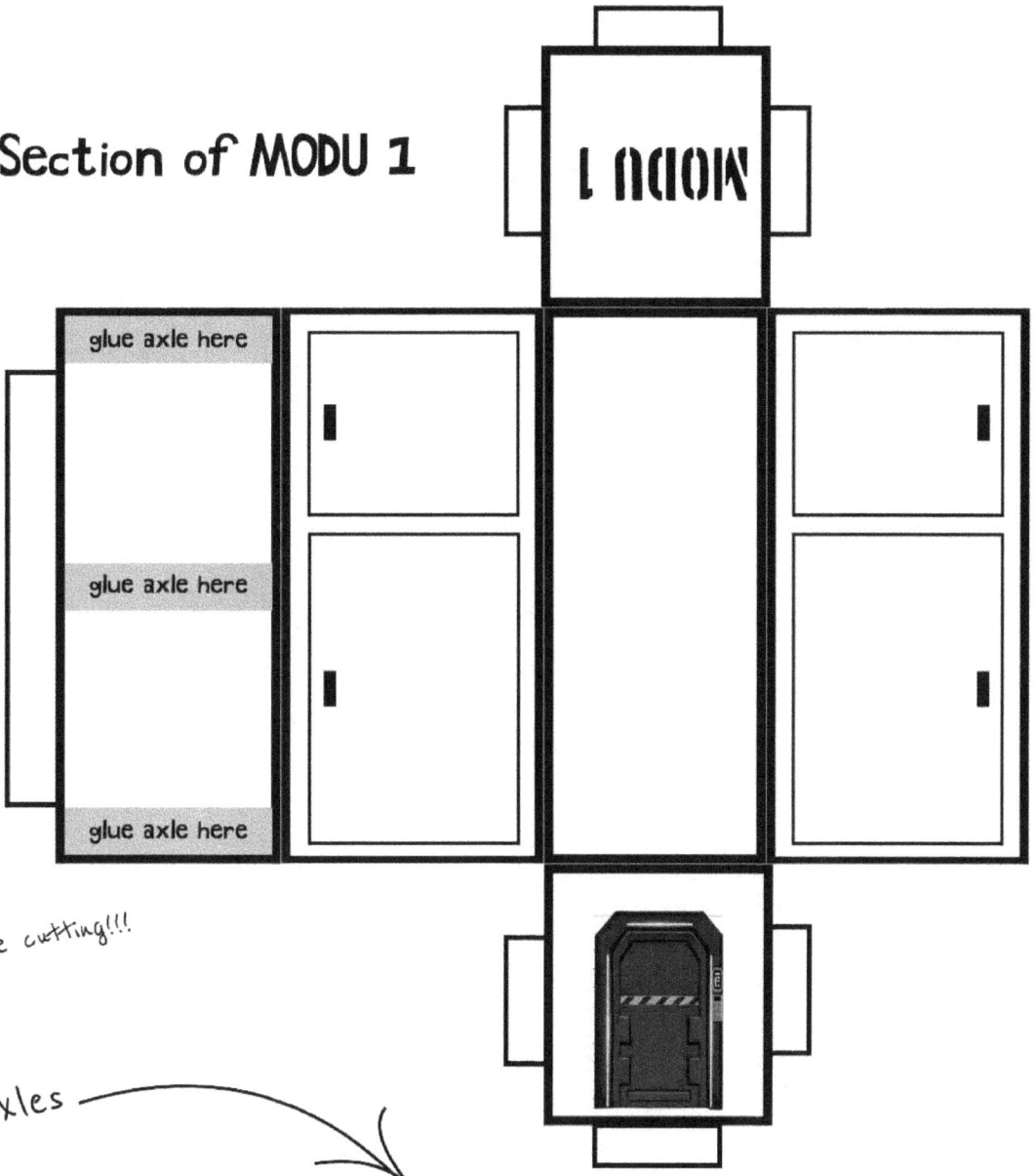

NOTE: Color before cutting!!!

The Axles

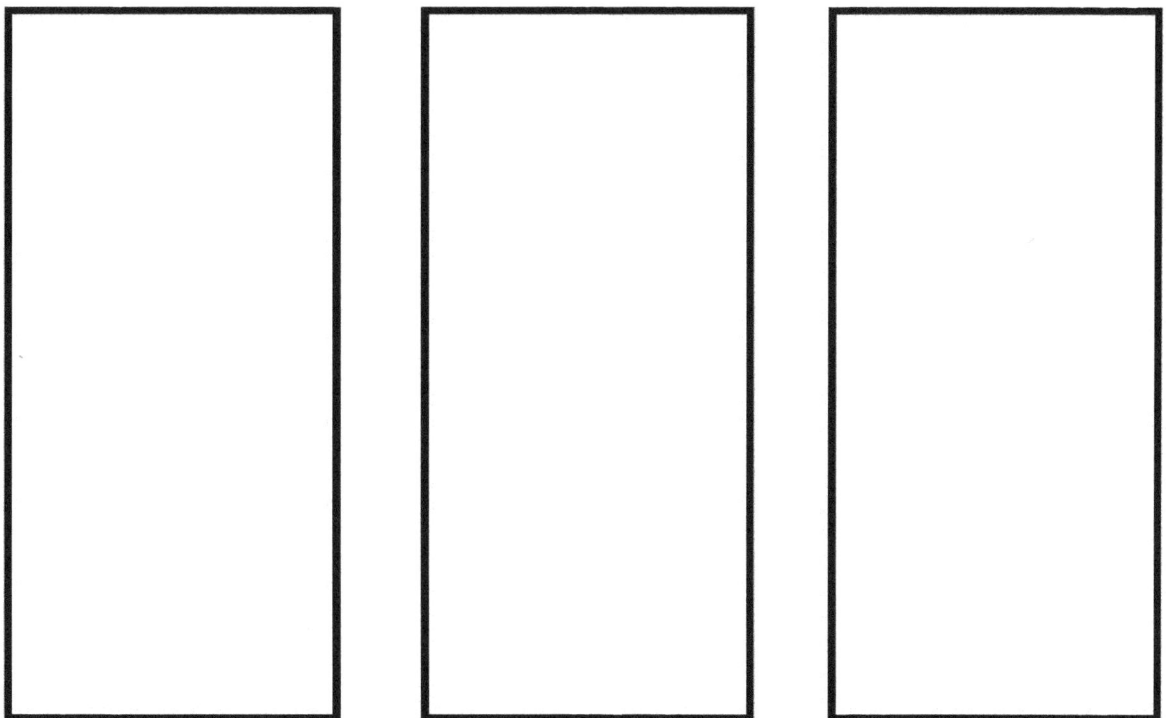

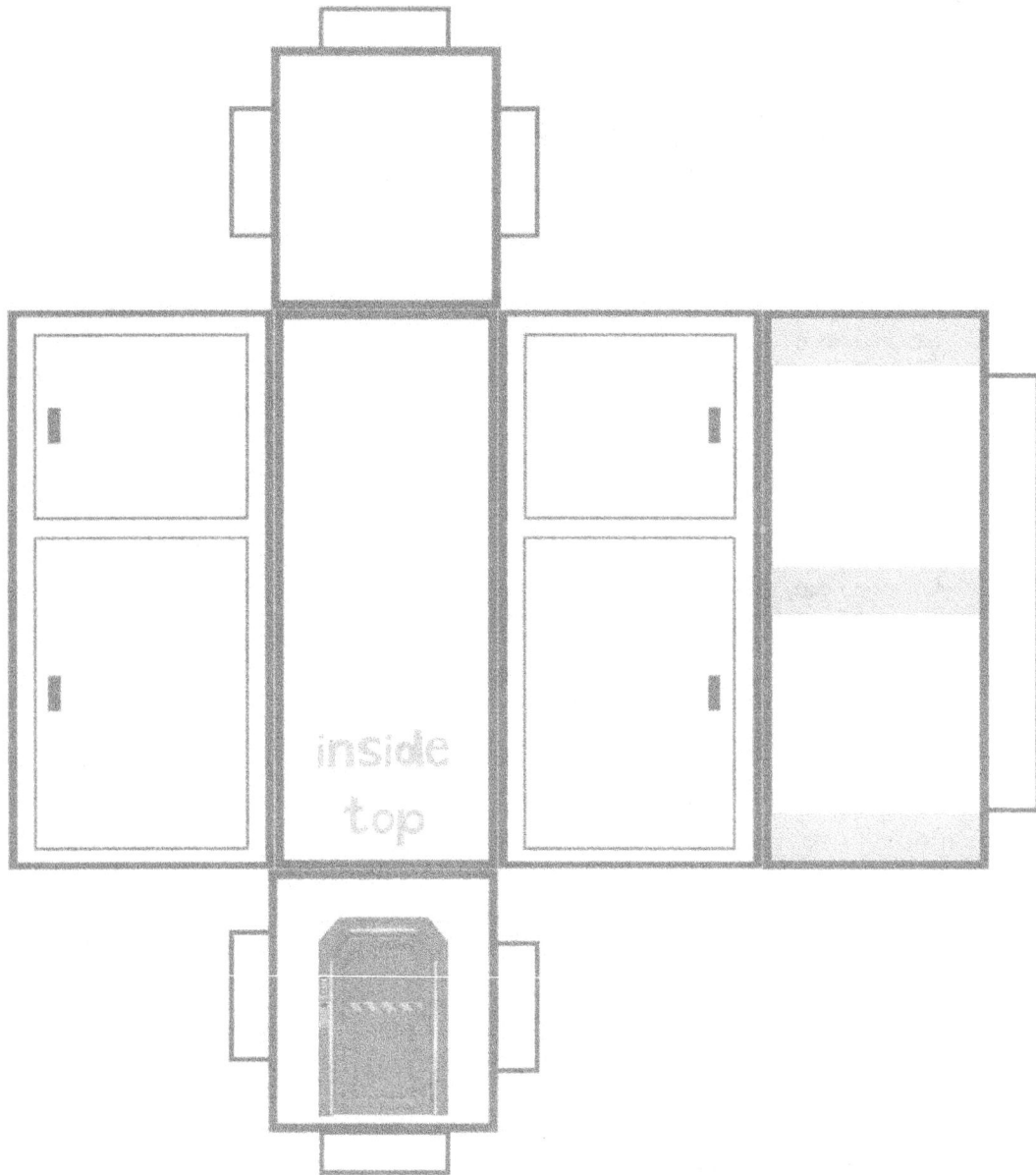

inside
top

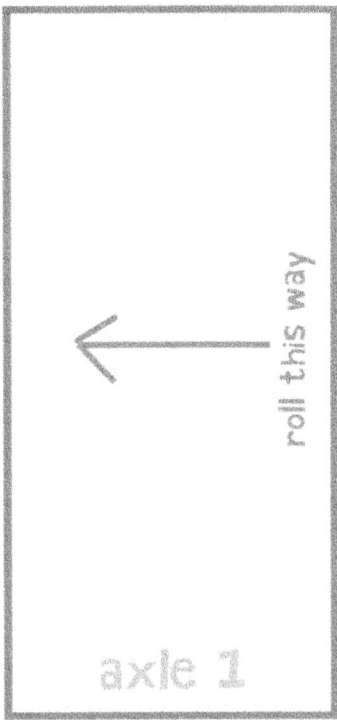

roll this way

←

axle 1

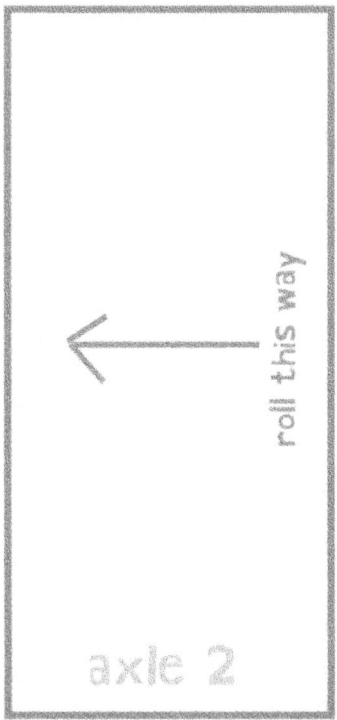

roll this way

←

axle 2

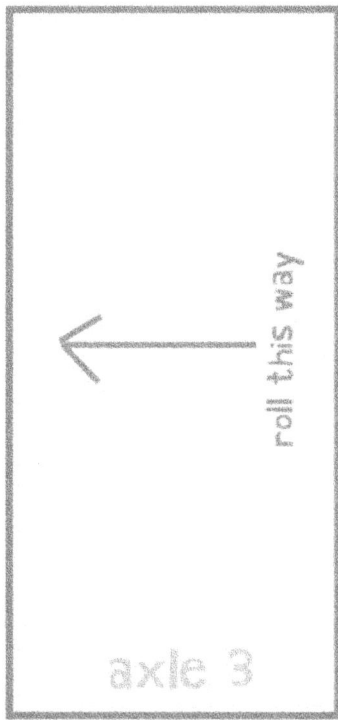

roll this way

←

axle 3

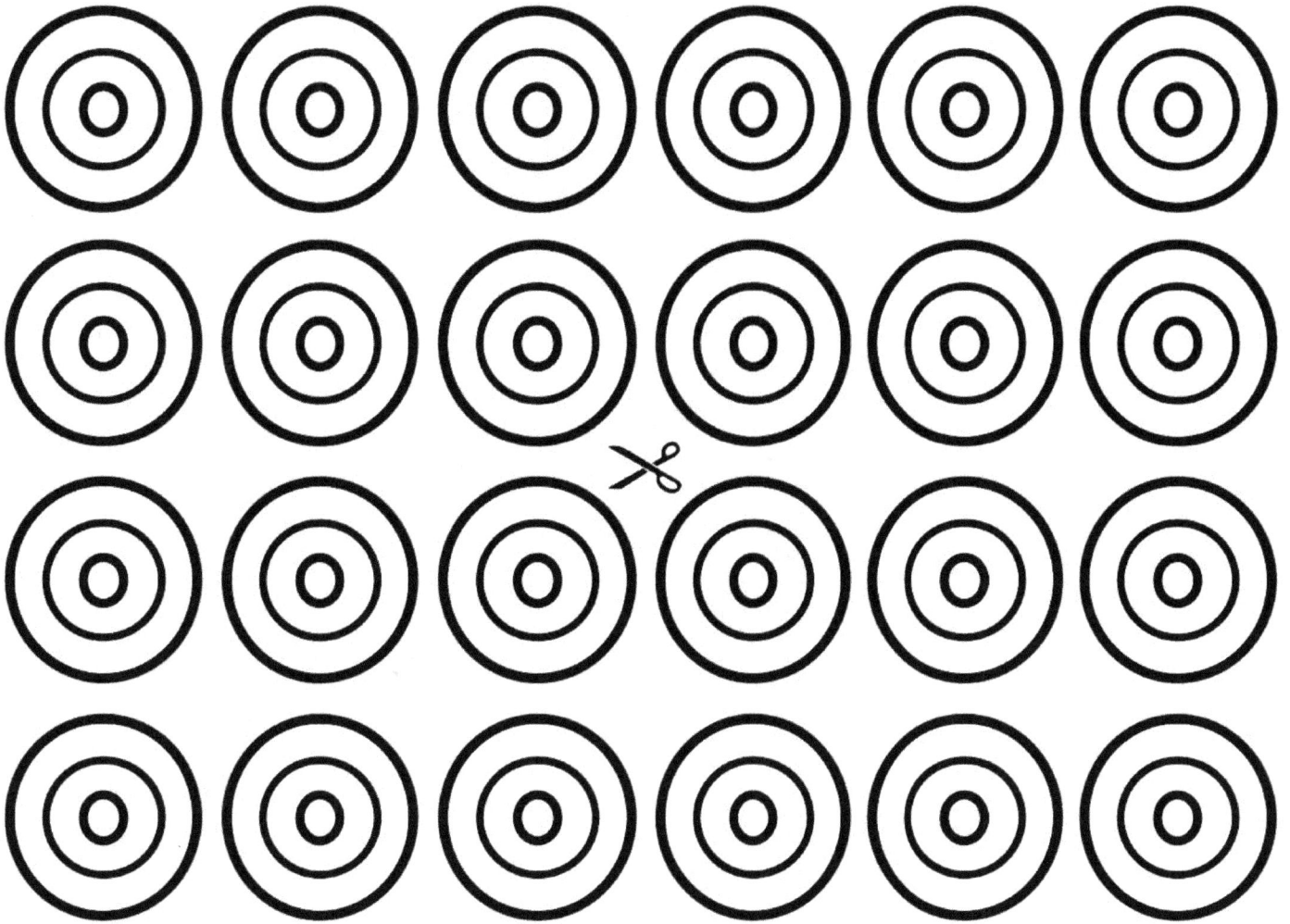

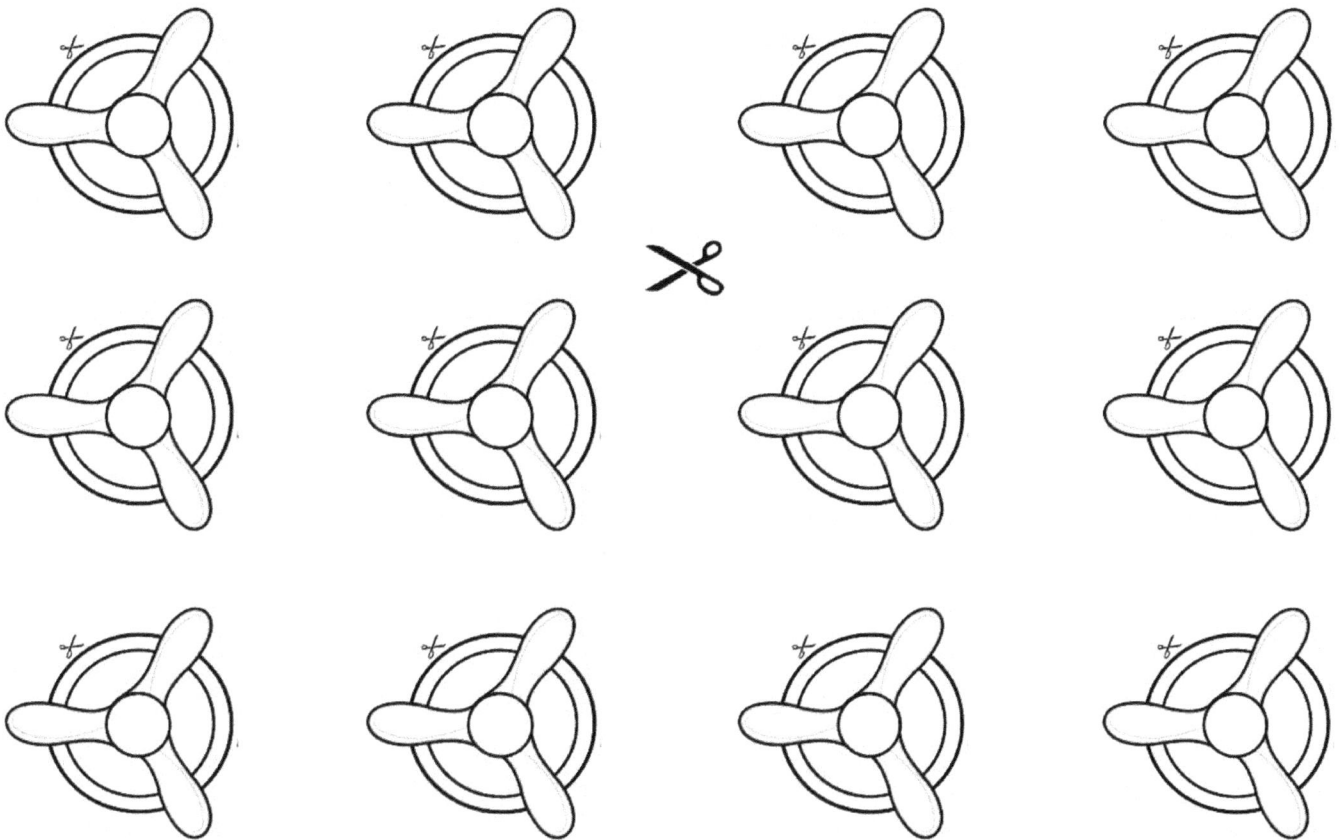

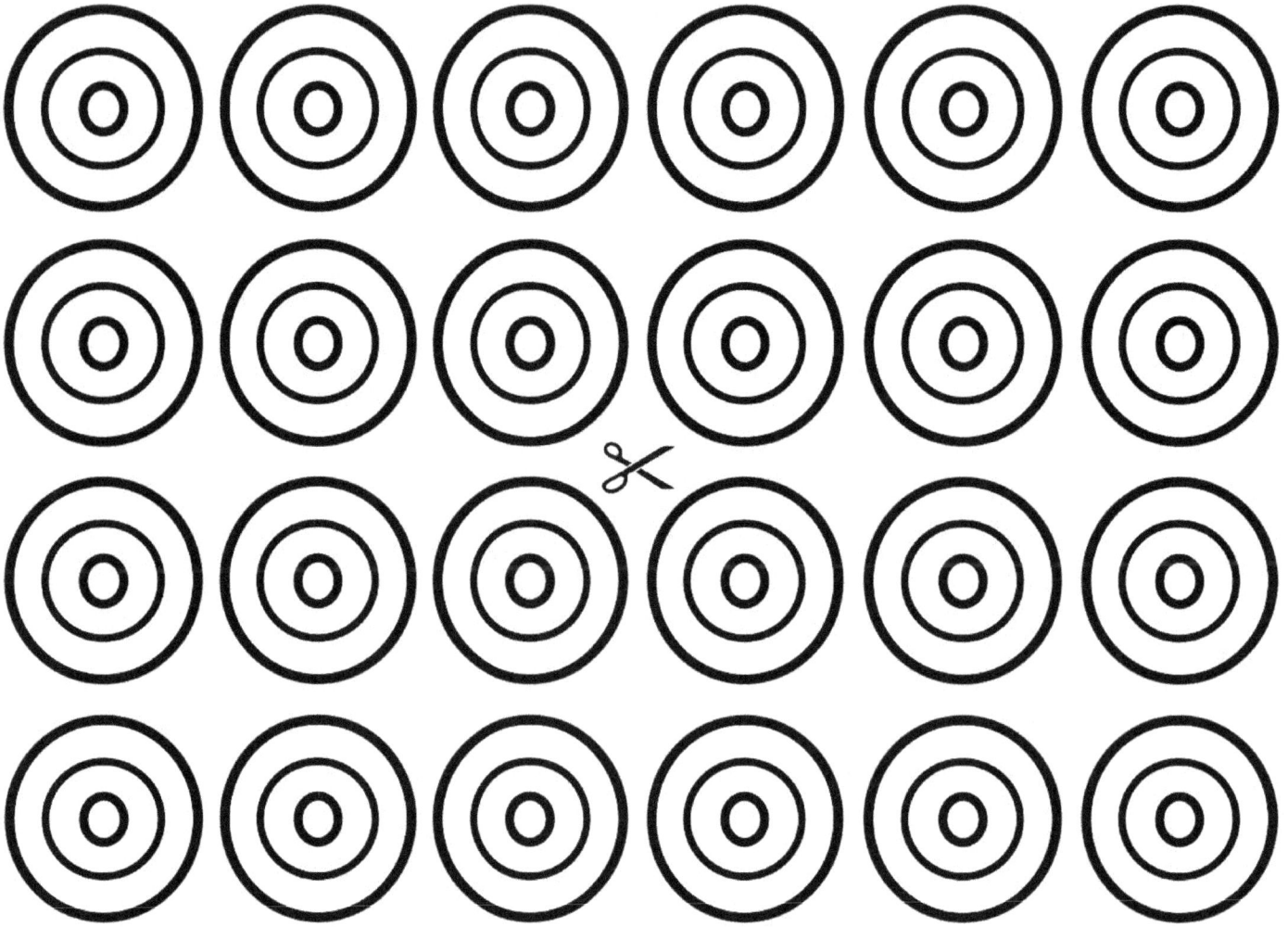

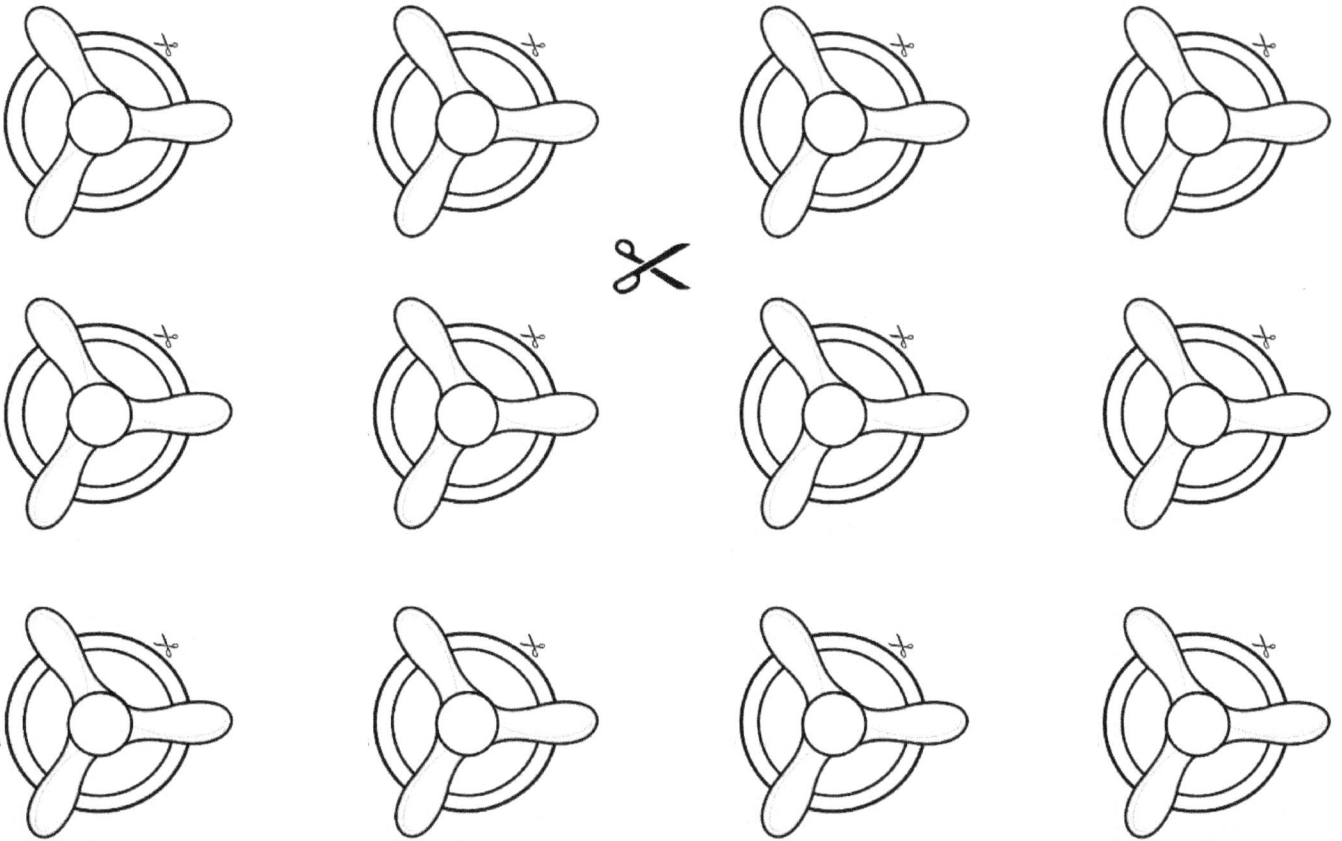

tire treads inside

tire treads inside

Top Section of MODU 3

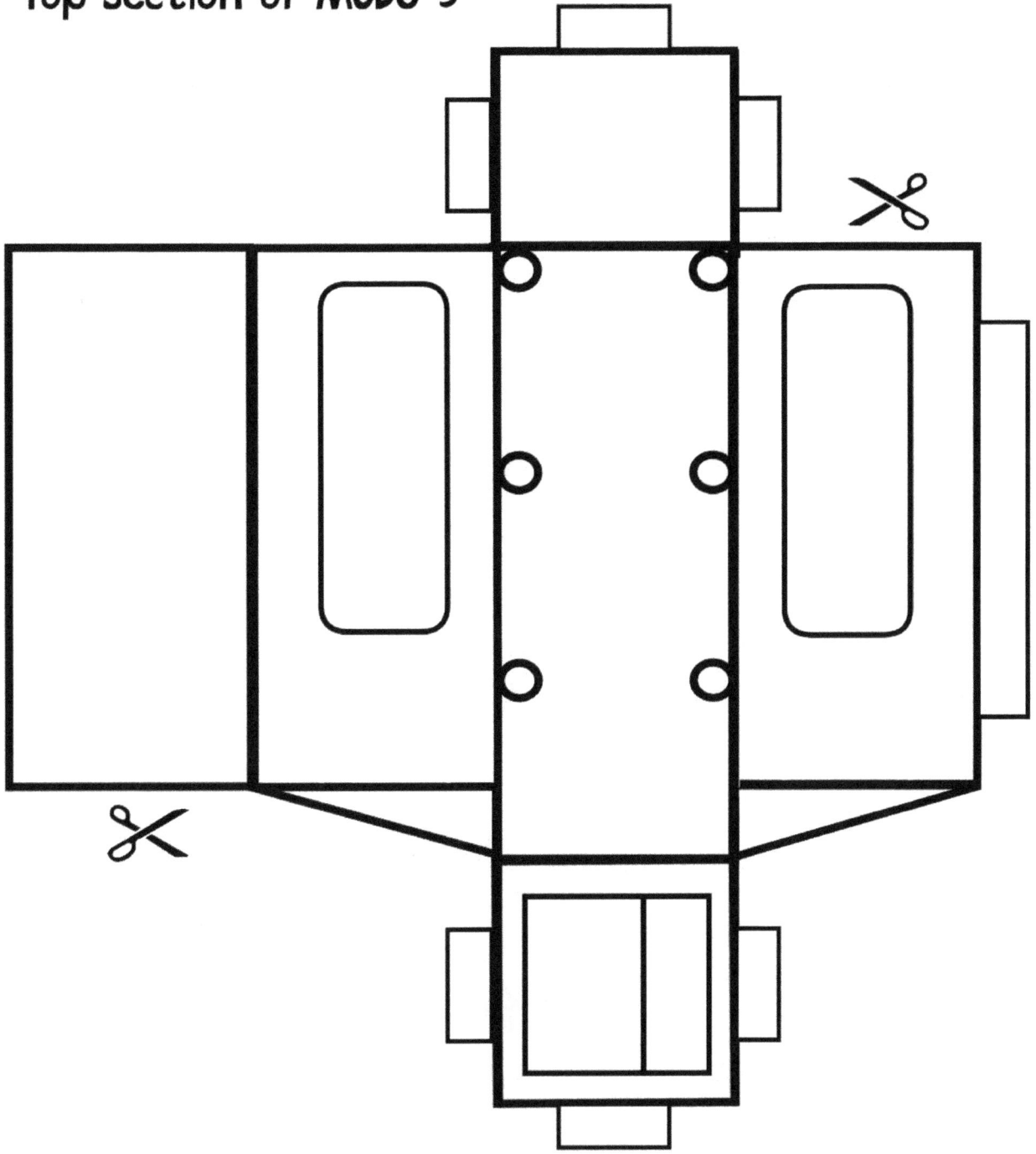

NOTE: Color before cutting!!!

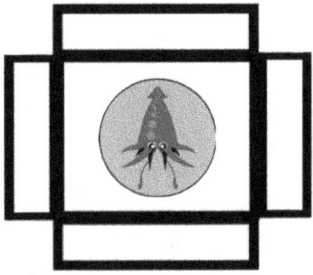

battery pack

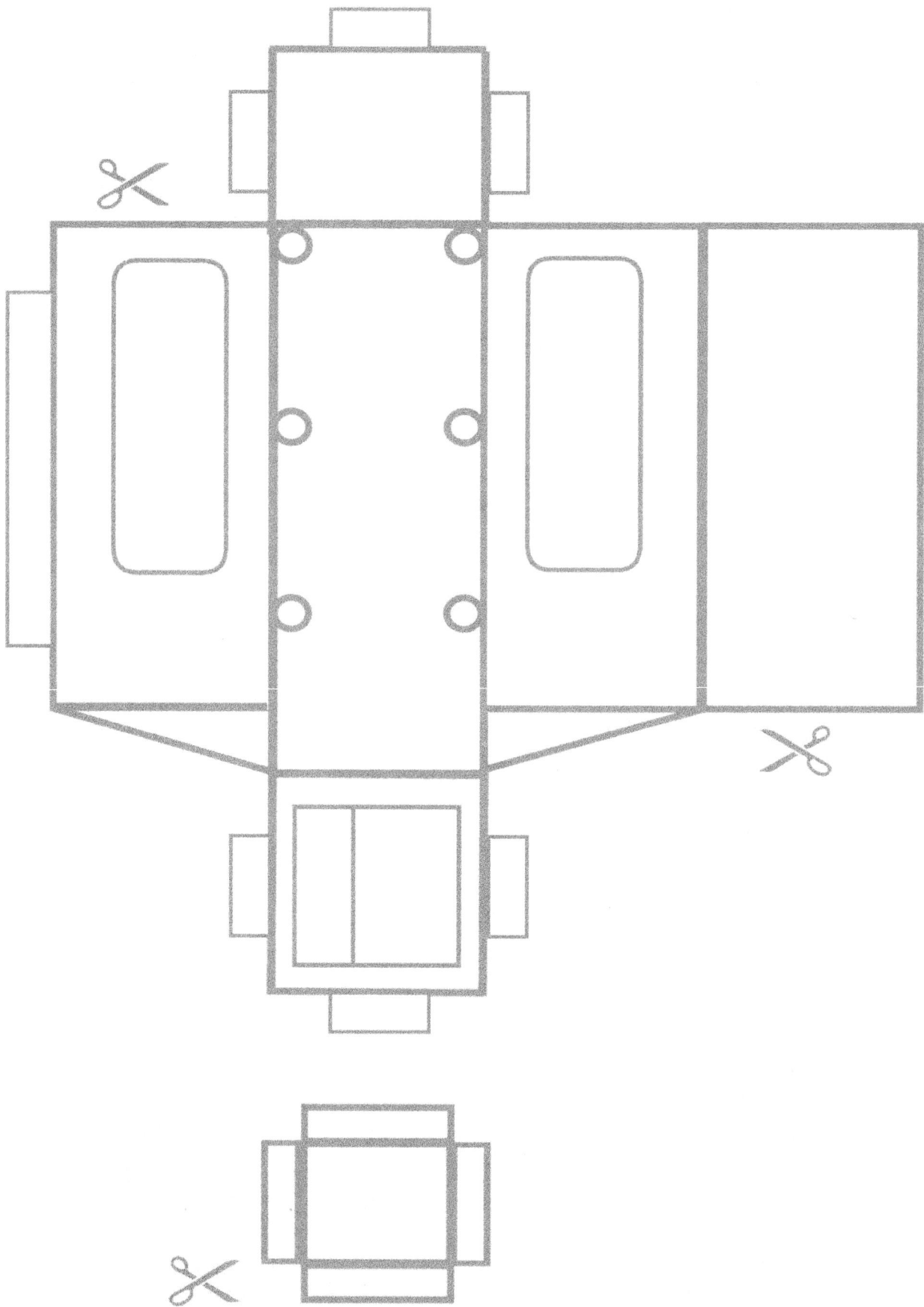

Bottom Section of MODU 3

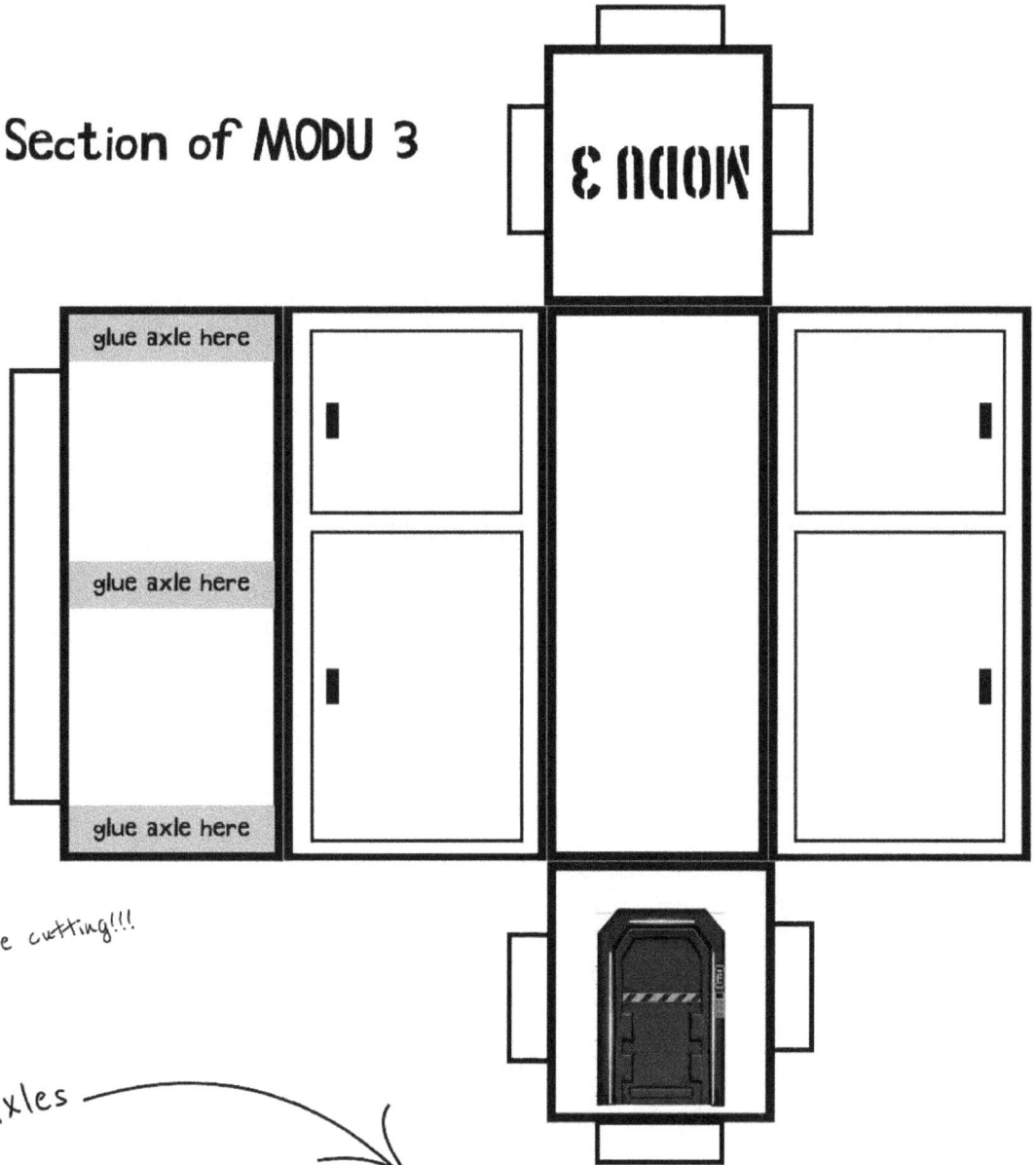

MODU 3

glue axle here

glue axle here

glue axle here

NOTE: Color before cutting!!!

The Axles

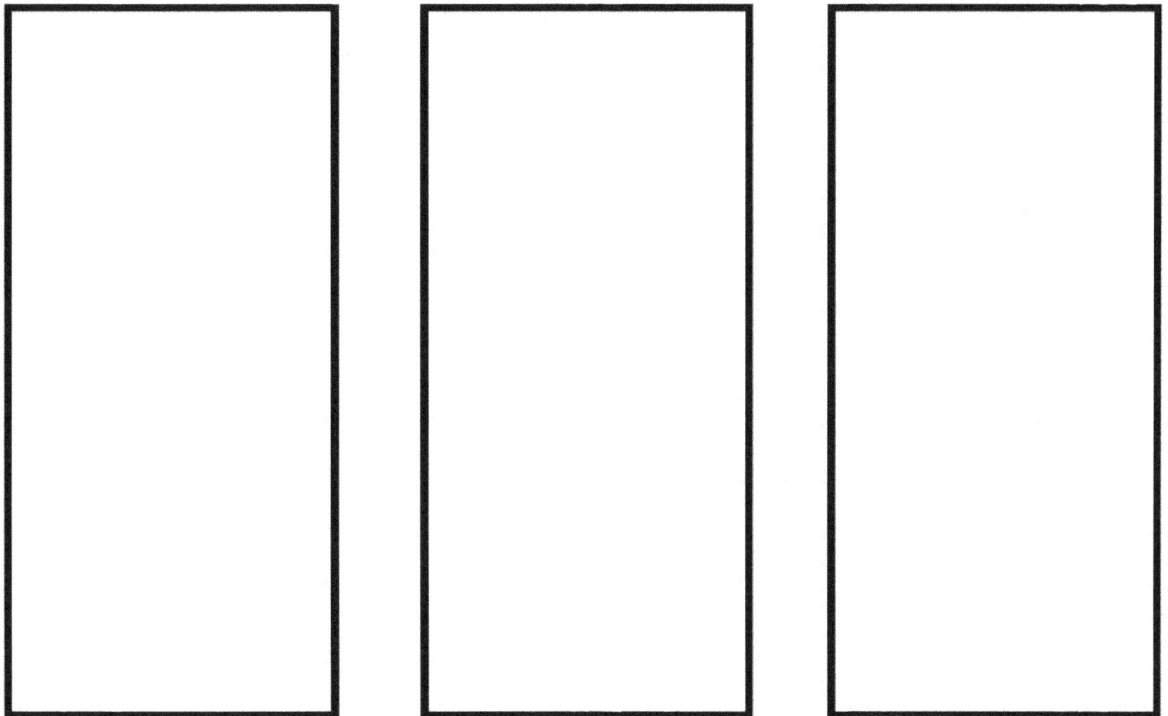

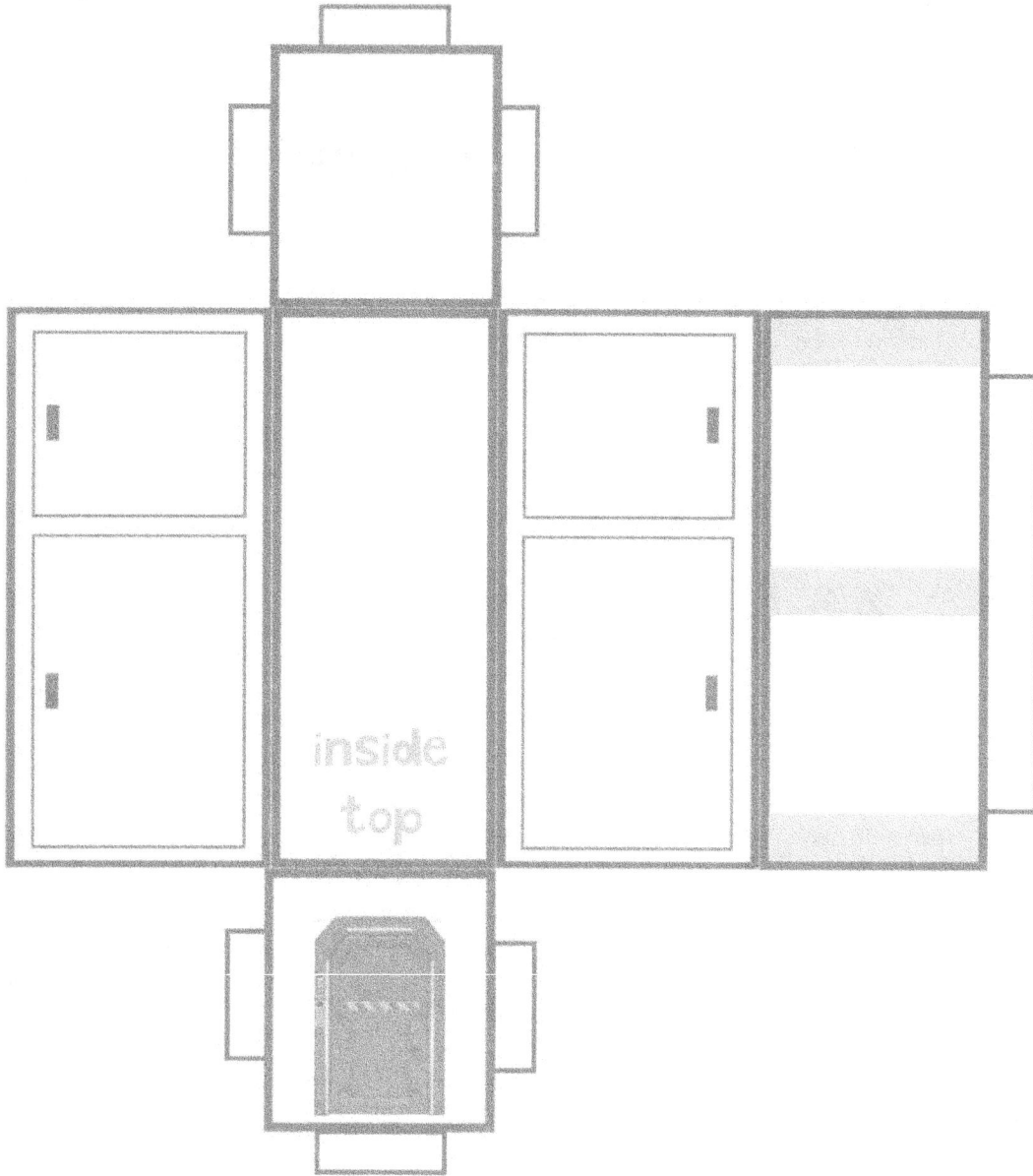

inside

top

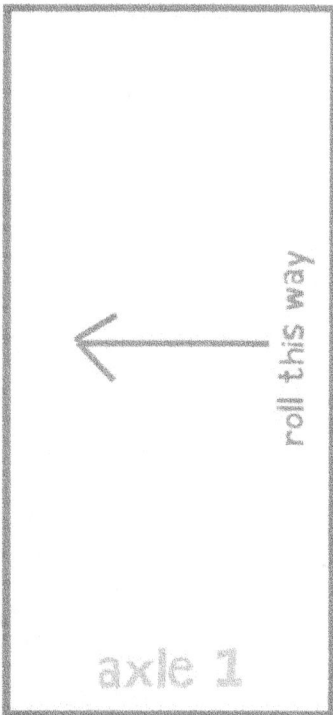

roll this way

axle 1

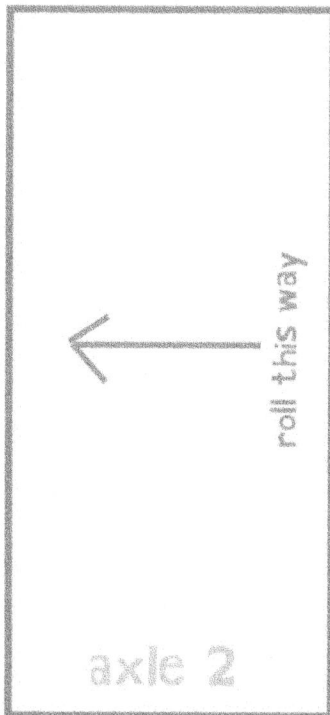

roll this way

axle 2

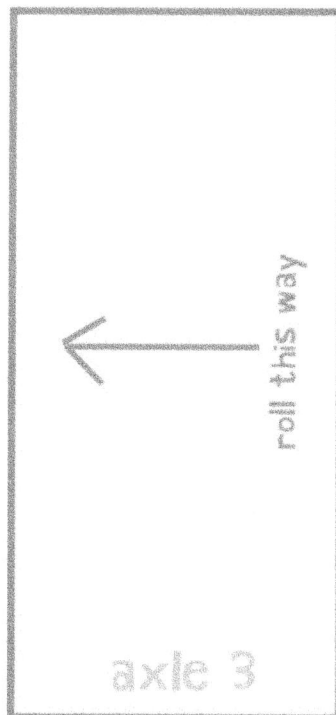

roll this way

axle 3

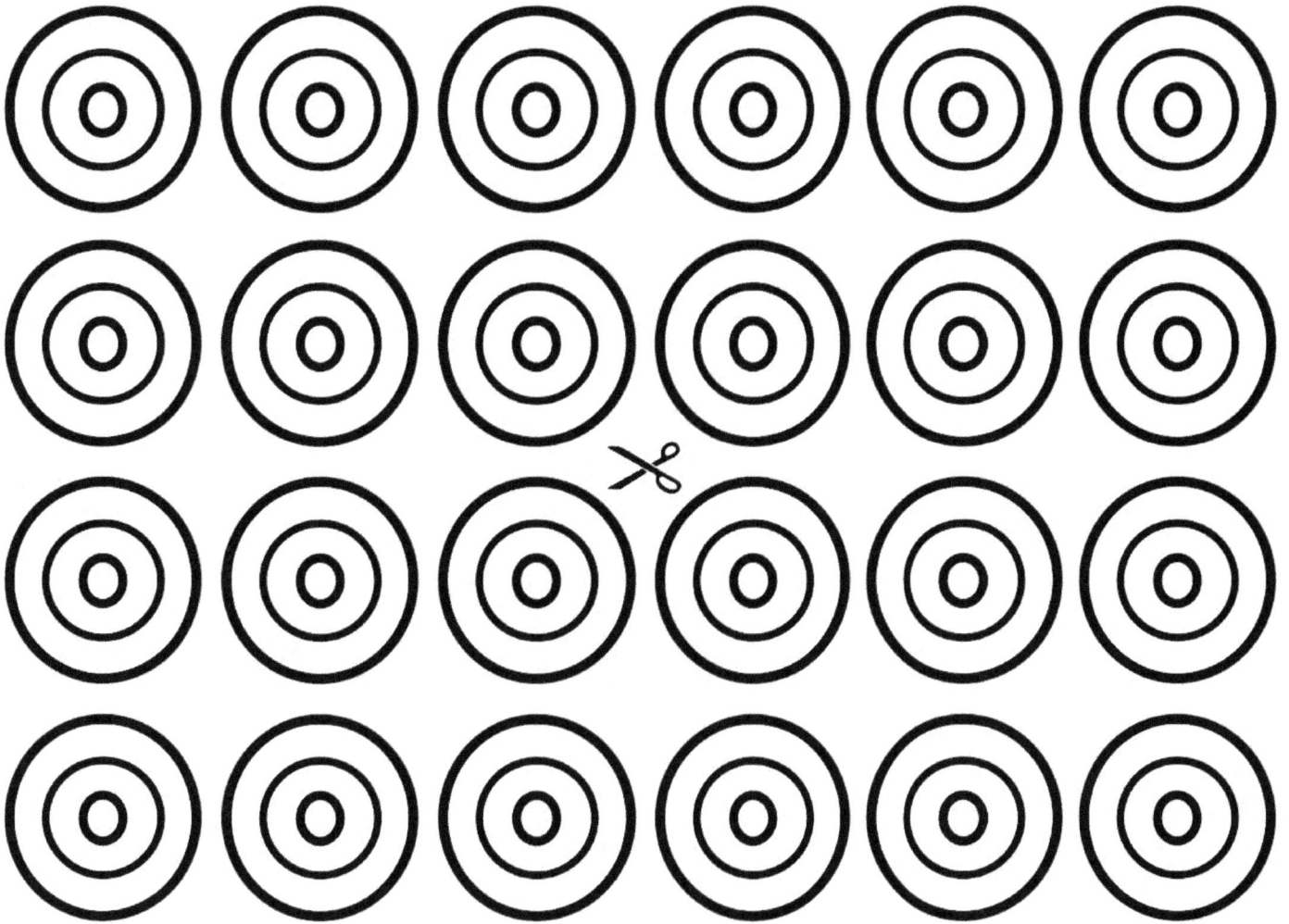

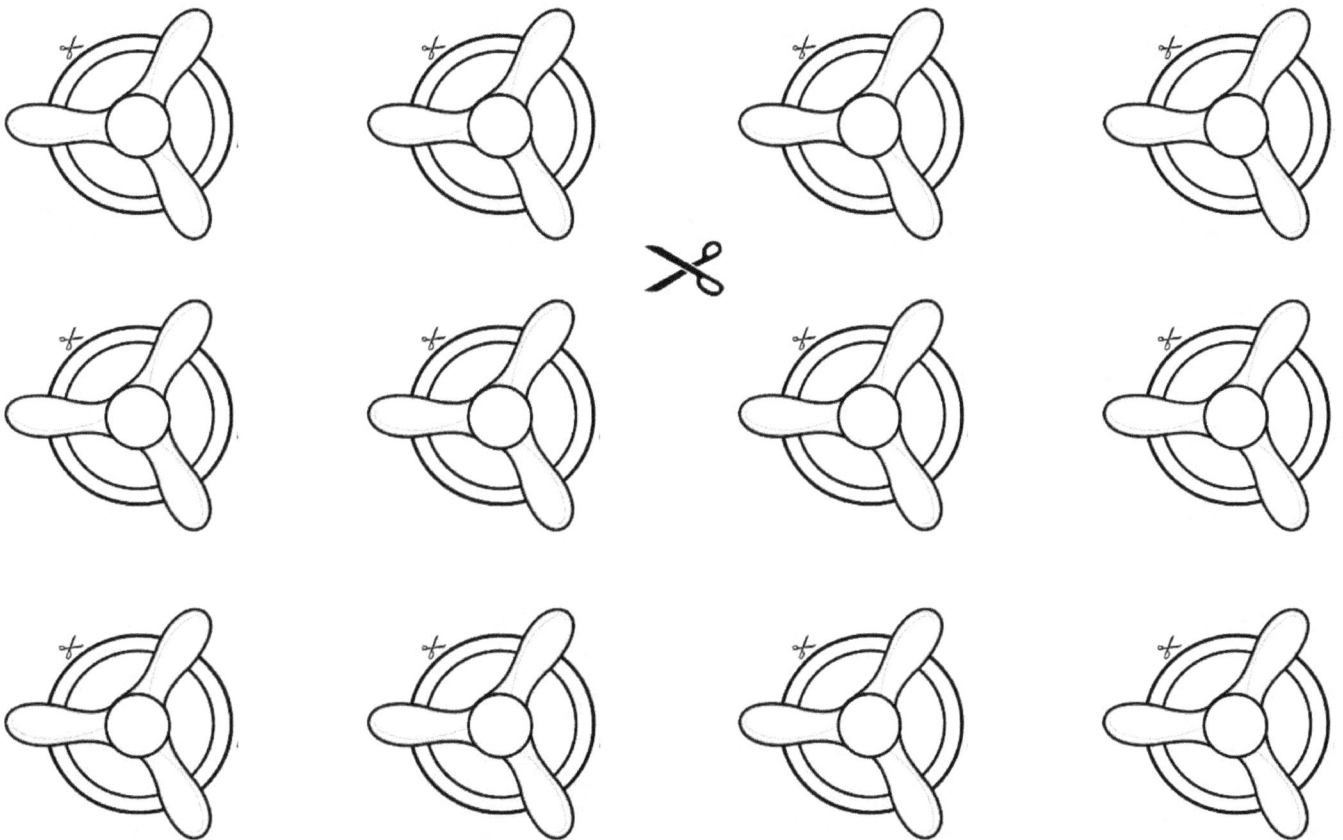

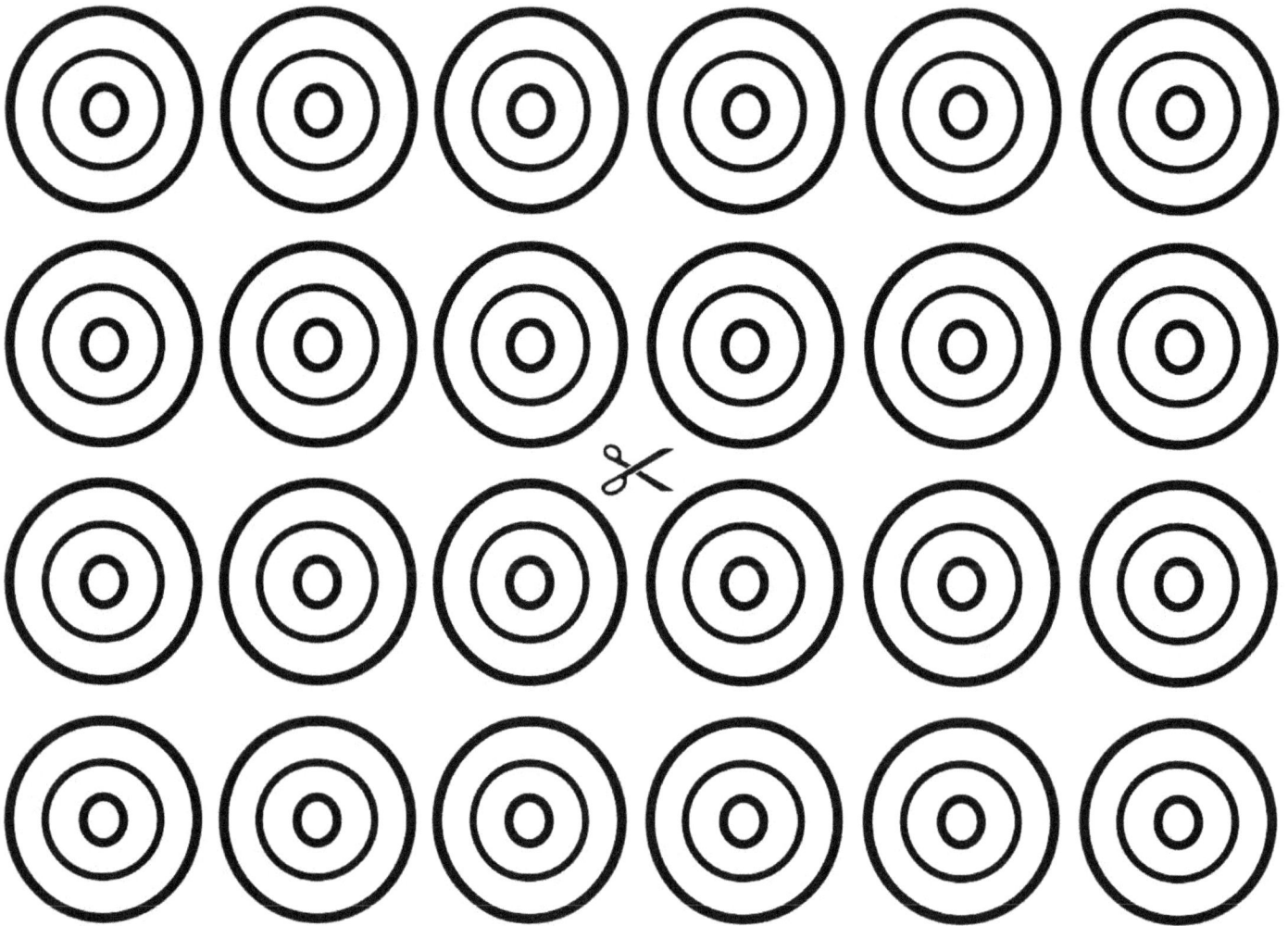

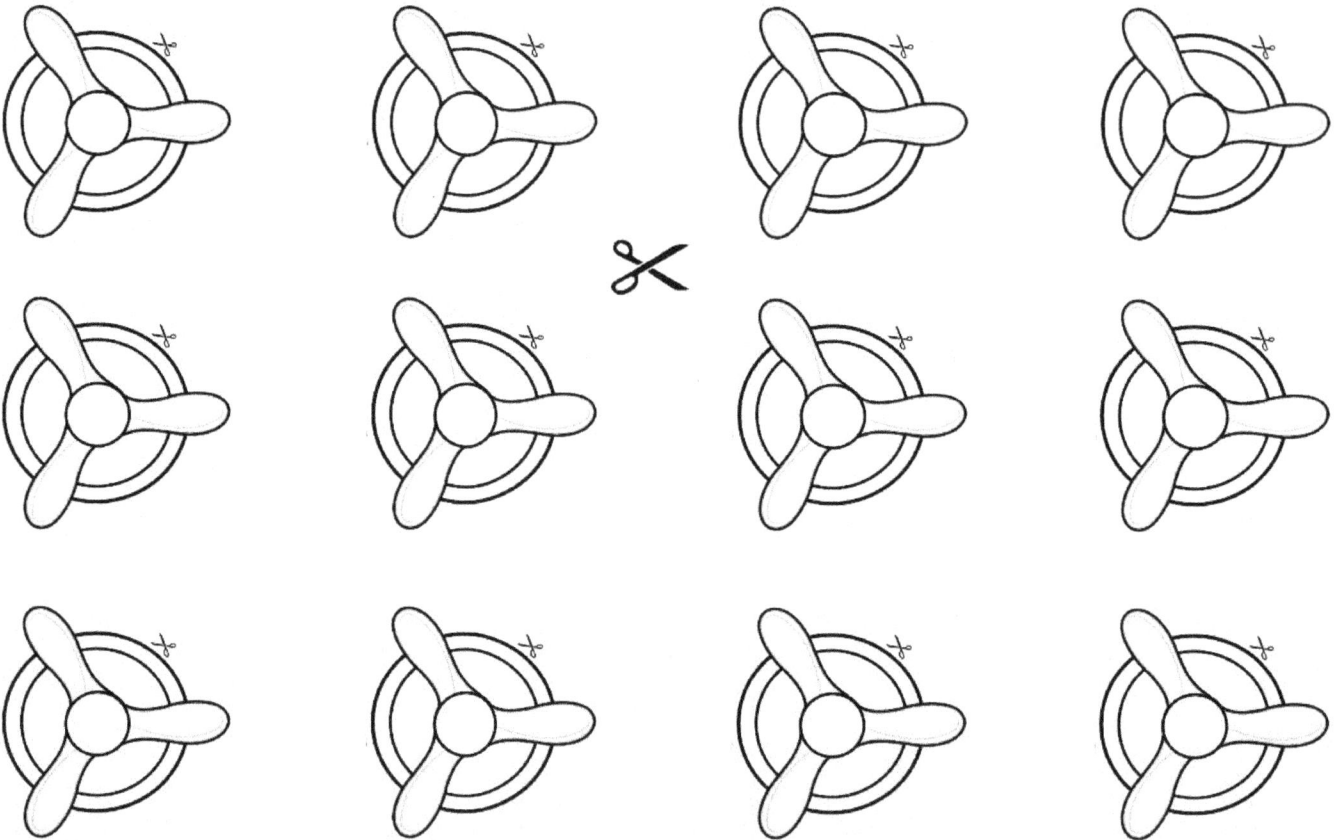

tire treads inside

tire treads inside

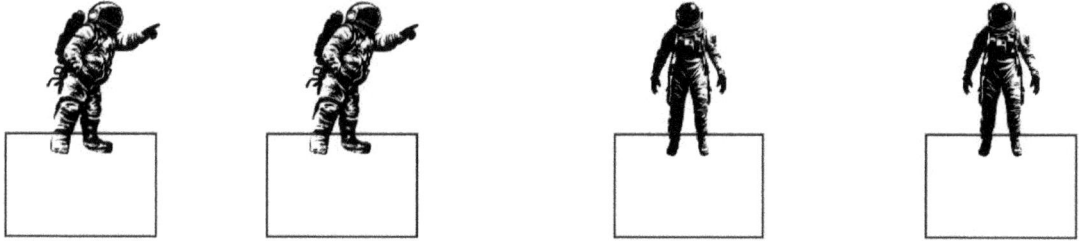

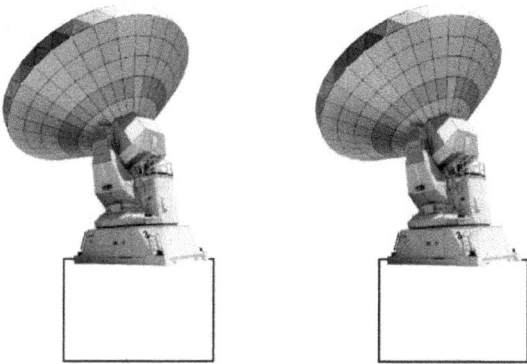

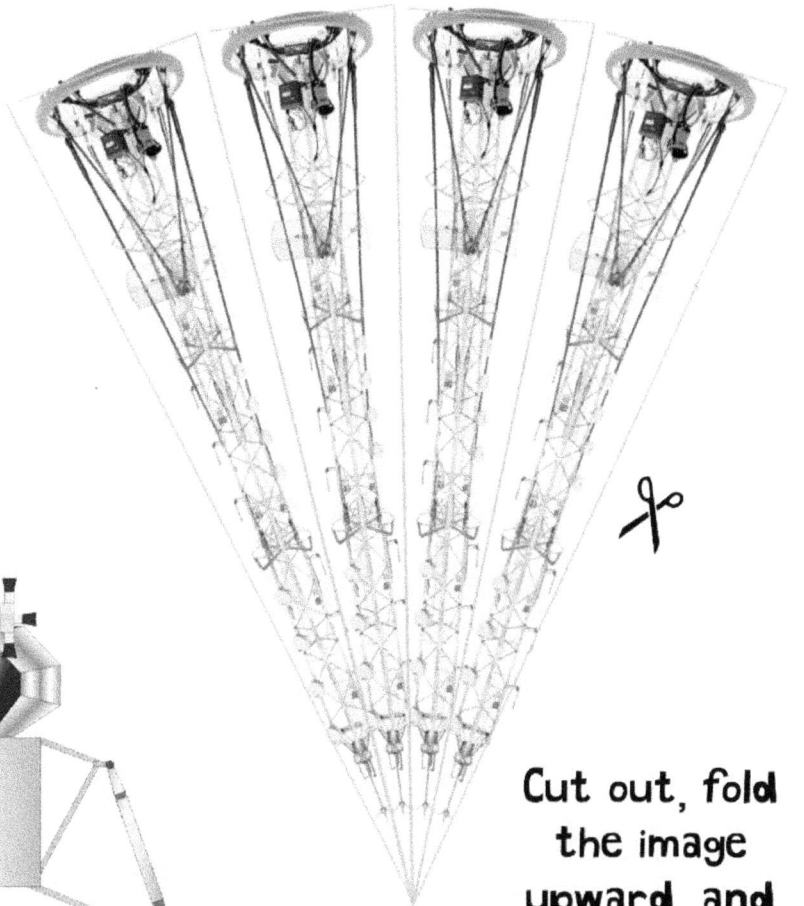

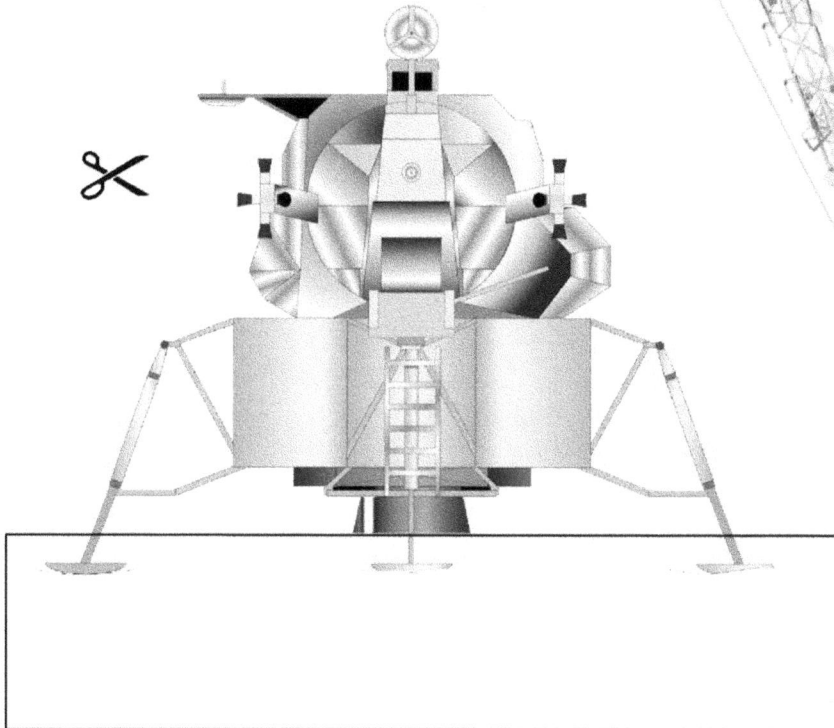

Cut out, fold
the image
upward, and
glue the
white
square
down.

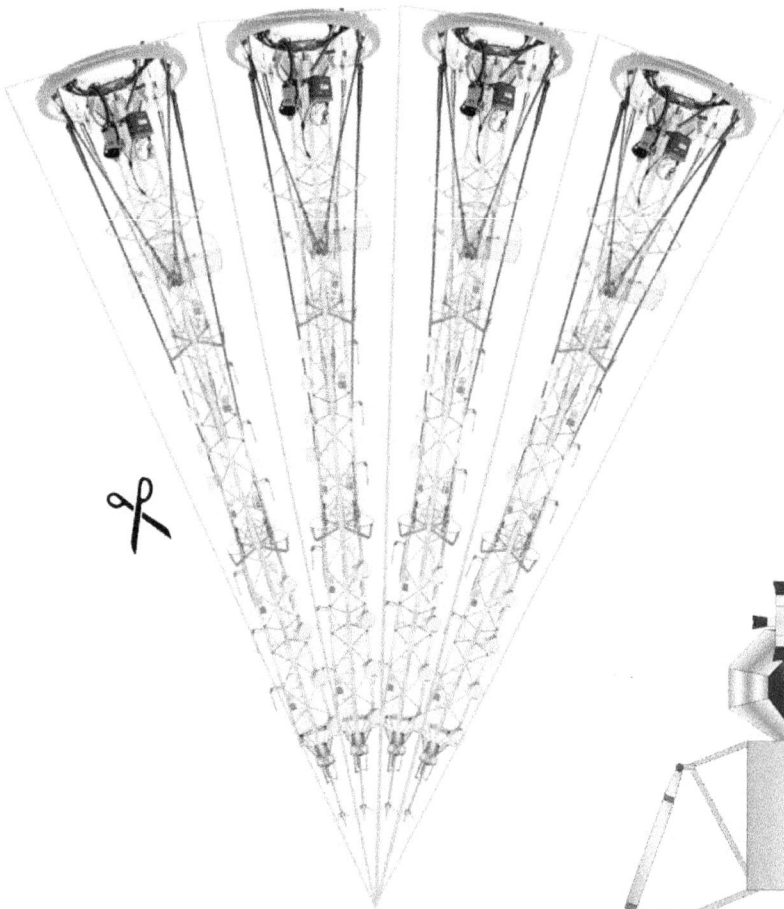

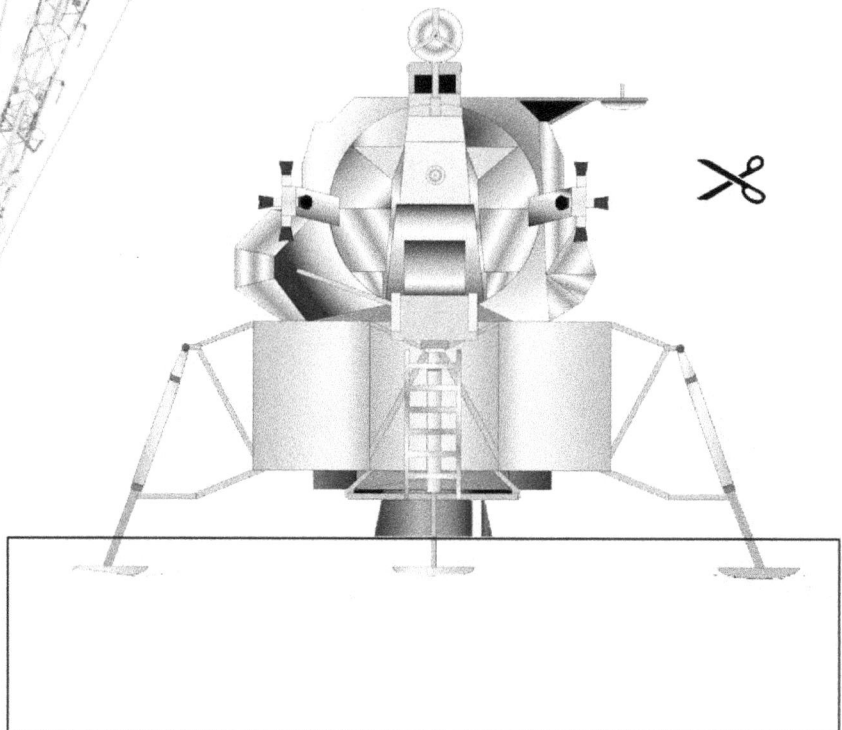

The Astronauts have finally arrived and brought the two Mobile Dwelling Units (MODU) with them.

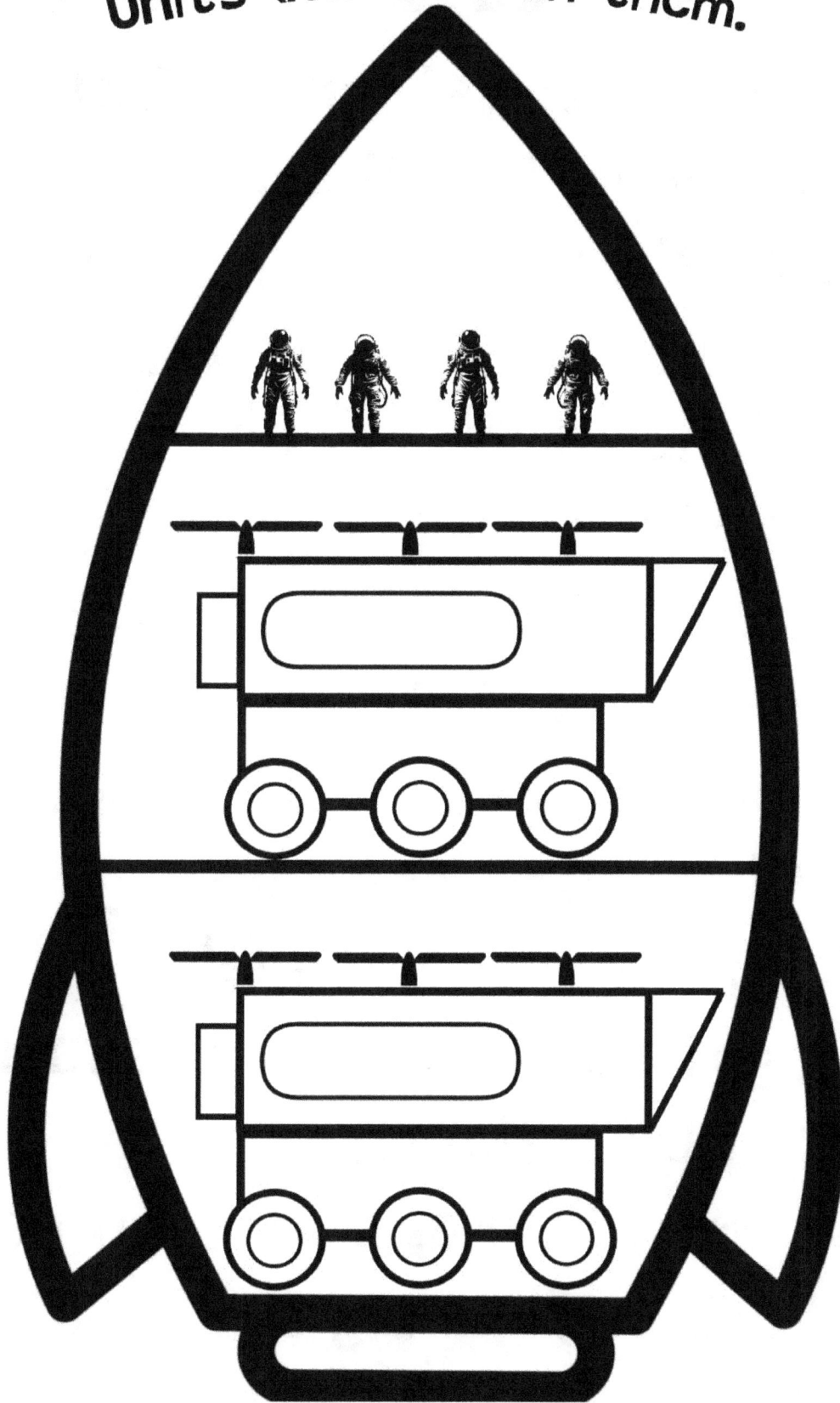

ALIENS!!!

When the four astronauts started to unload the MODUs on the surface of Mars, they noticed that the rocket engine melted the ice underneath it as they landed uncovering a strange-looking rock that had some odd-looking letters carved into it. Captain Harris, who is an expert in CRYPTIC Languages had determined the message must have been made by ALIENS. YIKES!!! He got some of the message figured out but can not figure out the rest. Perhaps you can help architect by figuring out what the rest of the message says.

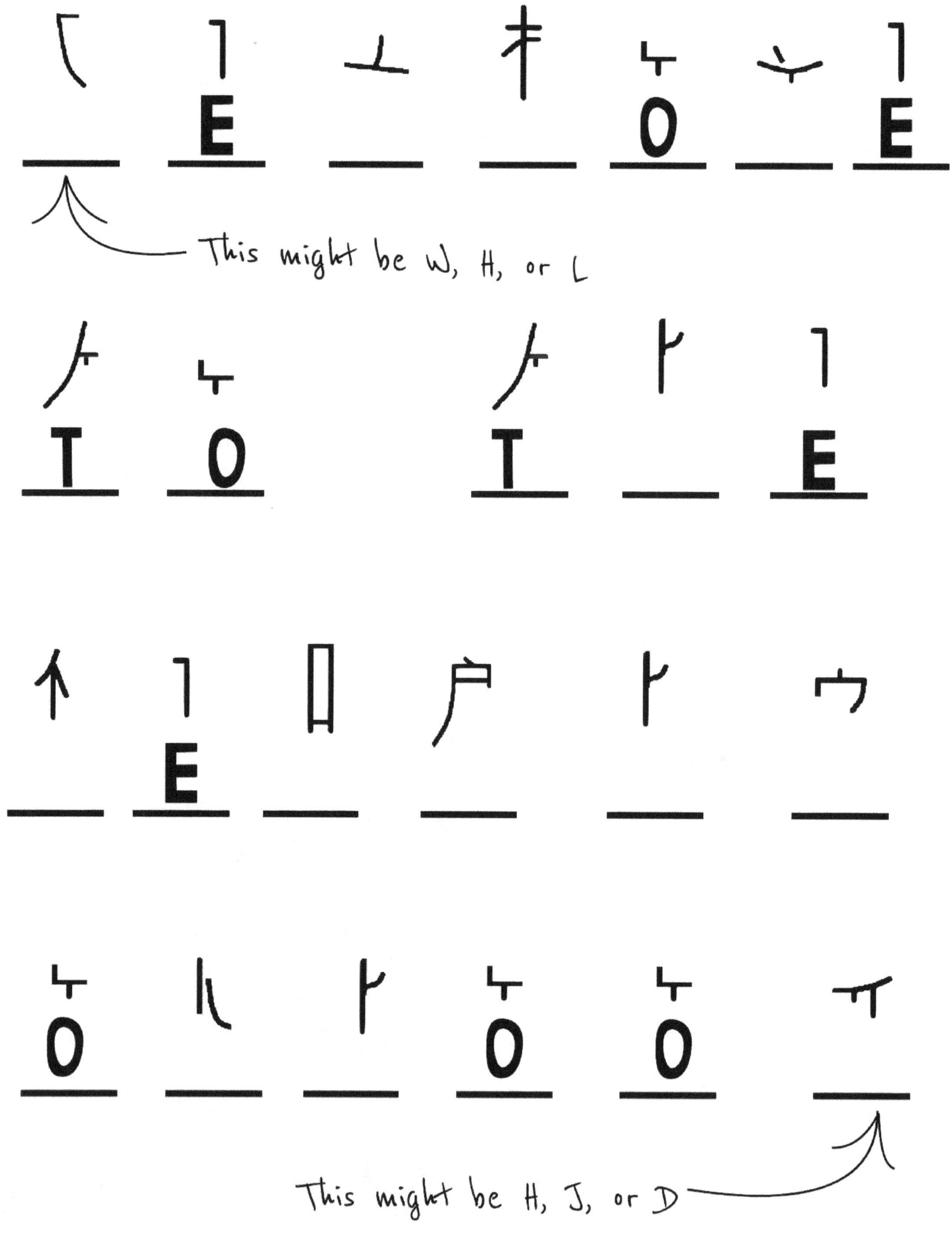

E   O   E

This might be W, H, or L

I   O   I   E

E

O   O   O

This might be H, J, or D

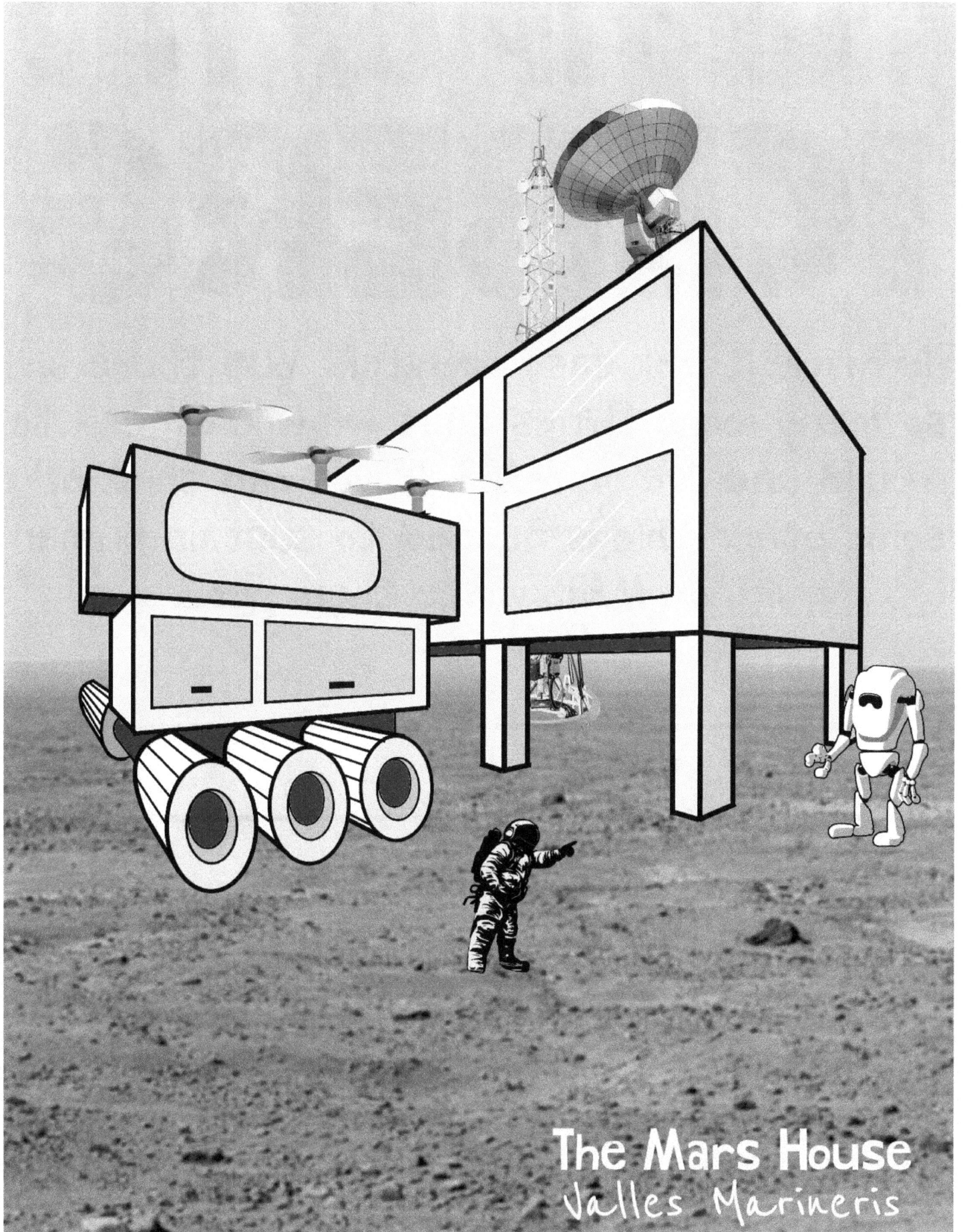

The Mars House
Valles Marineris

THE TIP OF THE
ICEBERG

We made it look easy architect but there are so many more things that we would need to build and live on MARS. If you can think of some other things needed to sustain human life on MARS write them here.

_____

_____

_____

_____

_____

...or perhaps you would prefer to draw your ideas. Do it here!!!

WELL DONE!

Congratulations architect on a job well done. We completed this house design project with our imaginations and architectural skills creating a beautiful design. We learned about the site location and took into consideration what our clients wanted, came up with a concept that fit those two things, and created a work of art. Not only did the clients love our design... the Society of Supercilious Architects gave us the prestigious "Pickle Prize For Architecture" award. Mine is already framed and hanging in the office, your award is over there on the next page. Stay tuned for upcoming projects architect, I'm gonna need your help again for another house design project somewhere in the ~~world.~~ Universe!

PICKLE PRIZE FOR ARCHITECTURE

This is to certify that

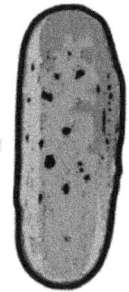

_____
(your name)

has been bestowed the coolest of cool, the wickedest of the wicked, and the raddest of the rad Pickle Prize for the best architectural design. An honor given to only the top architecture designs in the universe.

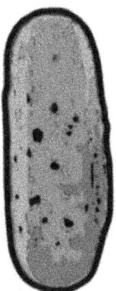

PROJECT NAME: _____

LOCATION: _____

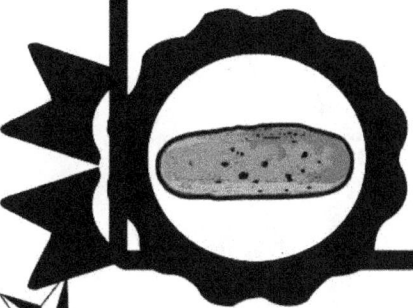

It was a difficult job architect but you did a really awesome job. Congrats on the award.

Albert B. Squid

Your mission to design a house on Mars for us was a complete success and we would like to thank you by making you an honorary Space Agency Astronaut. Congrats and come visit us anytime.

—Captain Harris Georgetown

ANSWER KEY

pages 24-25

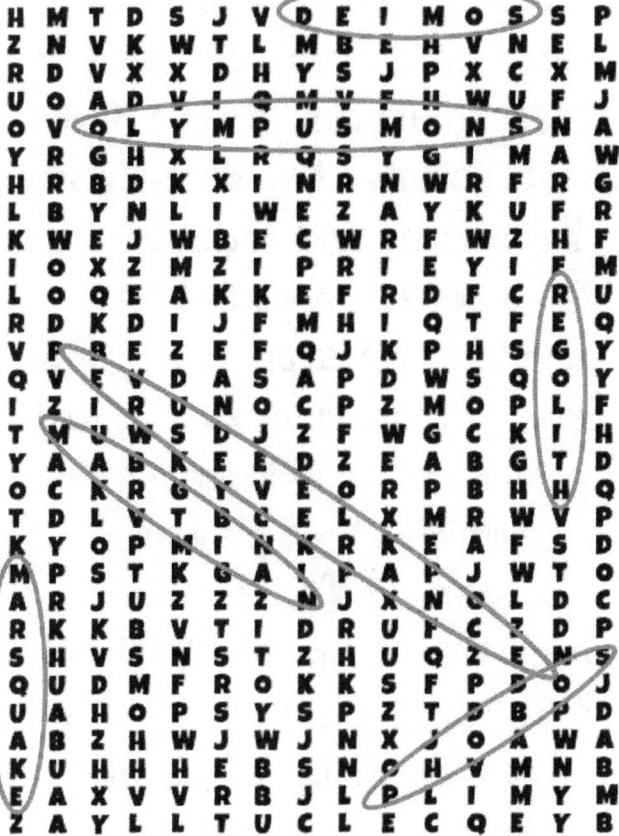

page 47

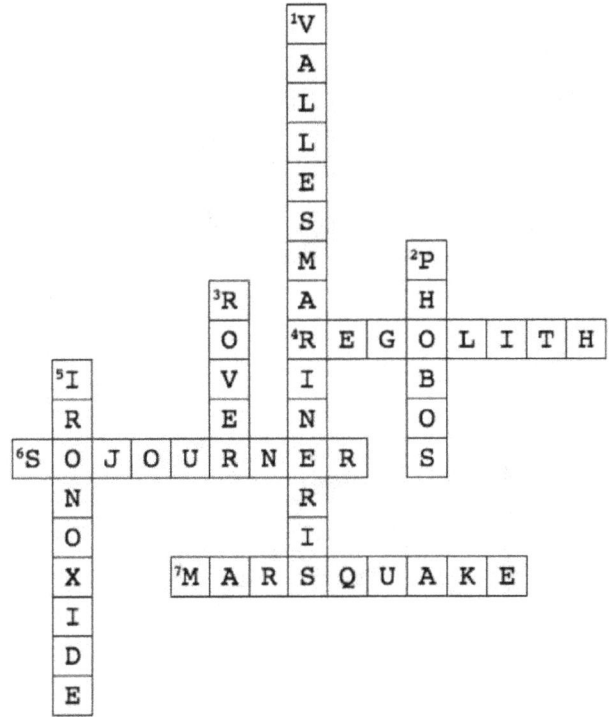

page 39

pages 129-130

WELCOME TO THE
NEIGHBORHOOD

ABOUT THE AUTHOR

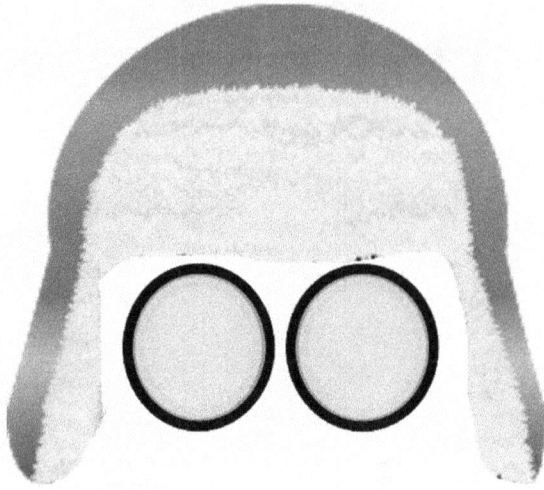

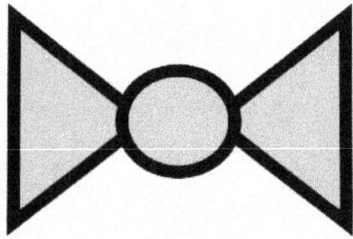

Born to a family of construction peeps, ALBERT B. SQUID was raised on construction sites in Massachusetts. Believe it or not, he holds two degrees in Engineering and Architecture and has worked as an Architect in Boston, Tokyo, and Seoul. In the year 2000, Squid started an independent children's book publishing company in NYC. I had fun doing that.....I mean HE (Albert B. Squid) had fun doing that! After becoming a freelance voice actor, the elusive author's whereabouts are unknown. He was last seen in the city of Jefferson, Indiana boarding a starship as he was holding a white rabbit and was talking to a woman about how the city of Jefferson was built on rock and roll. WHAT? WEIRD!

If you have a clue as to where Albert B. Squid might be, let us know at HQ by contacting us at:

info@squarerootofsquid.com

NOTE: Although Squid likes to stay out of the public eye, he should be easy to spot with his hat with flaps, mirror sunglasses, and funny bow ties.

LET'S DESIGN A HOUSE

with

ALBERT B. SQUID
Architect Adventurer

HOME

USA

KOREA

UK

CANADA

AUSTRALIA

SPAIN

UAE

"The lake monster did it!" My father's belly puffed up like a balloon, and a deep laugh that would've rivaled the bellowing of a massive beast escaped his lungs. "The nerve! To blame a silly, old legend on the disappearance of our materials and the changes in our plans. Nonsense! Ridiculous! Poppycock!"

"The legend of the Big Trout Lake Monster is very old," Jessica assured us. "People around here have been scared of the lake for years. No one goes on the lake or fishes in the lake, and no one lives on the lake."

"What about Mr. Wabash?" George poked his head around me in order to look Jessica in the eye when he asked.

"People think that the lake monster is actually his pet."

"Hogwash!" my father bellowed. "Tomfoolery! Balderdash! Such malarkey!"

"That's what the townspeople believe," Jessica further insisted. "My mother and father have been telling me stories about the lake monster for years. They say it's six feet tall with green gills and large fins on its hands and feet. It looks like a man, walks like a man, but it lives at the bottom of the lake and can eat a man whole if it's hungry enough."

39

albertbsquid.com